Xmas/Birthday 2023

Kayla

♡

Praise for *Lighter*

"yung pueblo is the real deal—a modern sage and guiding light. In his new book, he beautifully illustrates how finding harmony within is the key to creating a progressive society built on compassion, clarity, and understanding. This is a book everyone must read, many times over."

—Vex King, #1 *Sunday Times* bestselling author of
Healing Is the New High

"yung pueblo teaches how to heal with compassion as the driving force. *Lighter* is an empathetic and wise book that will guide you on a journey toward a deeper understanding of self and help you make impactful changes within and in the world. yung pueblo created a core curriculum on how to heal despite your experiences with suffering."

—Nedra Glover Tawwab, LCSW, *New York Times*
bestselling author of *Set Boundaries, Find Peace*

"A beautiful encouragement for tending your own heart: for learning and healing, for finding well-being, and being part of the solution for all you care about."

—Jack Kornfield, author of *A Path with Heart*

"To learn of yung pueblo's beginnings in this intimate book is a gift. *Lighter* helps us understand the daily ways in which his deepening practice has impacted an entire generation of seekers. His words leave an indelible mark—his struggle with self-abandonment and his personal process of compassionate self-connection have quietly inspired millions of us. yung pueblo's humble, potent teachings help us prioritize our emotional maturity in the face of constant change, a vital understanding in these turbulent times."

—Elena Brower, bestselling author of
Practice You, Being You, and *Art of Attention*

Lighter

Lighter

Let Go of the Past, Connect with the Present, and Expand the Future

yung pueblo

HARMONY

BOOKS • NEW YORK

Library of Congress Cataloging-in-Publication Data
Names: Yung Pueblo (Writer), author.
Title: Lighter : let go of the past, connect with the present, and expand
the future / Yung Pueblo.
Description: First edition. | New York : Harmony Books, [2022]
Identifiers: LCCN 2022001517 (print) | LCCN 2022001518 (ebook) |
ISBN 9780593233177 (hardcover) | ISBN 9780593233184 (ebook)
Subjects: LCSH: Self-actualization (Psychology) | Emotional maturity. |
Mental health.
Classification: LCC BF637.S4 Y86 2022 (print) |
LCC BF637.S4 (ebook) | DDC 158.1—dc23/eng/20220126
LC record available at https://lccn.loc.gov/2022001517
LC ebook record available at https://lccn.loc.gov/2022001518

ISBN 978-0-593-23317-7
Ebook ISBN 978-0-593-23318-4

Printed in the United States of America

Book design by Andrea Lau

4th Printing

First Edition

Contents

pick the path that lights you up
the one you know deep down is the right choice
stop listening to doubt
start connecting with courage
do not let the idea of normal get in the way
it may not be the easy path
but you know great things take effort
lean into your determination
lean into your mission
lean into the real you

people who have experienced deep suffering
and are still gentle with others
do not get enough credit
to not let the hard things
that happened to you win is heroic work,
to drop the bitterness
and still live with an open heart
despite it all
is a massive gift to the world

My Story

As I lay there on the floor, crying tears of fear and regret, my mind took on a sharpness that for the first time allowed me to see how far I had veered from my potential—how I had allowed drugs to block me from having to deal with my inner sadness.

I had been recklessly pushing my body and mind with dangerous excess when I finally pushed myself too far. It was during the summer of 2011, after another night blindly focused on the pursuit of escape and pleasure, that I found myself on the floor, thinking my heart was going to explode. I was twenty-three and convinced that I was having a heart attack. I was both scared I was dying and embarrassed that I had let myself get to this point.

My mind flashed back to my teen years, working as an activist and organizer for the Boston Youth Organizing Project (BYOP). I remembered how nourishing it had felt to be part of a group helping others reclaim their power and making real change. How had I lost my path?

In the beginning, I thought I was just having fun and that I was in control. But I could now see that the partying had become a way for me to avoid spending time with myself. I used and abused drugs to numb the pain and hide. There was sadness and anxiety inside me that screamed for my attention, but all I could do was turn away from it. And my drive to keep my attention away from my emotions stood like a wall blocking me from considering the long-term impact that drugs would have on my well-being, on my life.

My mind also kept focusing on the bravery of my parents, how much they had to sacrifice and how hard they had to work to give me, my brother, and my little sister a better life in the United States. When I was four years old, we moved to the United States from our home in Ecuador. Being immigrants and trying to make it in our new city of Boston left its mark on all of us. In the long run, it was the right decision to move here, but for the first decade and a half we all felt the intense pressure of poverty. It almost broke us. My mother cleaned houses and my father worked in a supermarket. It was a miracle that they made ends meet, but too often it was an incredible struggle that placed them under an immense amount of stress. Even though we lived simple lives with zero luxuries in a small two-bedroom apartment, money was still always lacking. As I lay on the floor, I kept thinking to myself, "I don't want to die this way. I don't want to let my parents down. They have worked so hard and selflessly, given so much to me, that this would be a horrible way for me to die. I need to live and make the most of the opportunity they have given me."

For about two hours I just lay on the floor, unable to move, as I felt the shock that my body was going through. I prayed and begged for my life, as I kept bouncing between regret and gratitude. Regret for slowly losing the drive to serve others and for not figuring out earlier how to handle my inner tension in a healthy way. Gratitude for the strength of my parents and their ability to take care of me and my siblings under such challenging conditions, for their selflessness and their unwavering love. Most of all, I felt an enormous pull to cling to life and begin again so that I could make the most of all the energy my parents had put into giving me the chance at a better life.

The movement between regret and gratitude reignited the fire of life in my body. After a few hours, my heart stopped beating so intensely and I no longer felt as if my life were on the brink of ending. My body felt incredibly fragile and exhausted from trying to remain in the realm of the living, but even so I got myself back on my feet. I had one clear objective. I grabbed all the self-prescribed "painkillers" I had and threw them away. That day, I resolved deeply in my heart to stop dulling my senses and to start the long walk back to a better life. *Gambling with my life, just because I feared my emotions, was over.* I knew that I had to cut out all the drugs and start being radically honest with myself.

I did not yet understand what was happening inside me and why I had fallen into such bad habits, but I knew that part of the reason was that I was lying to myself about how I really felt inside. I didn't know how I would finally heal, but I instinctively knew that my path forward had to be based on radical honesty, having the strong determination to stop ravaging my health with dangerous intoxicants and focusing on building new healthier habits for my body and mind.

It was a hard and long journey back to health, but slowly the changes started. I knew it was not going to be easy, I knew that good habits would feel like entering an unknown world, and I knew the only way to walk through it would be by taking each step with bravery and determination. But I was done with hiding.

During the years when I had abandoned myself, my mind felt undeniably heavy, and I knew that I needed to find a clear way to help feel lighter. I began by examining every part of my life and put my focus on doing the opposite of what had almost led me to an early death, from eating foods that made me physically stronger to exercising to paying real attention to my thought patterns, even when they felt turbulent. I started examining my relationships with friends and family and tried behaving with kindness and patience in areas where there was once too much roughness and irritability.

I acted like a detective in my mind, asking questions to deeply investigate and discover the source of my problems. Whenever the urge to escape with intoxicants tried to take hold, I would bring my awareness inward to take a good look at the tension. I remember finding immense amounts of sadness and fear, and an emptiness that ached for love. Later I would discover that this was a space that only my own love and unconditional compassion could fill. I did not immediately arrive at answers to all my questions, and it was not until I started meditating that I learned the real root of my suffering. But the simple act of being unafraid to take a deep look within released much tension in my mind. Simply accepting whatever I found helped me feel a new sense of ease, even when my mood was down. Running away from myself took up so much more energy than mustering the courage to embrace solitude and stillness.

The first year of building positive habits created a massive shift in my life. I did not feel terrific immediately, and every day was not a good day. Most days felt like a huge struggle. From the work of sitting intentionally with an emotion that scared me or just the mundane task of waiting in the cold for a bus to take me to the gym, staying committed was not easy. It all felt new and difficult. There were many ups and downs during that time, but my persistence did not waver. Going back to how things were was no longer an option. The habits that initially felt like impossible tasks started slowly becoming second nature. And as time passed, happiness became more common and my heart started feeling stronger. No matter how stormy my emotions got, bits of joy began appearing at random. I kept up the practice of turning inward to take a good look at what was bubbling up inside me, and, once the changes in me started adding up, I noticed that my relationships with family and friends were also improving. The old feeling of heavy, stagnant energy started lifting. Before the healing, I felt like a stranger inside my mind and heart. Gradually, that feeling passed and I began to feel at home in my own being.

Though life already felt new, and the learning felt continuous, when a friend told me about Vipassana meditation in 2012 I knew intuitively that this was something I needed to pursue to take my healing to the next level. *Vipassana* means "to see things as they really are." These are silent ten-day courses that teach you how to purify the subconscious mind through self-observation.

The healing began as soon as I initiated practicing radical honesty, but much deeper levels of healing opened up when I took up meditating. As I progressed in meditation and attended silent courses a few times a year, not only did I begin to feel better, but I started to feel freer. It took a while for me to be able to meditate consistently at home, but when I made a full commitment to meditating daily, starting in

2015, the positive changes in my mental health flourished. By 2016, I stopped consuming alcohol and marijuana and adopted a lifestyle that was free of all intoxicants. I felt like the two were making my mind dense, while meditation was trying to make my mind lighter.

Turning inward by practicing meditation felt like an intimate and personal renaissance. I started learning so much about myself and the human mind. Closing my eyes to feel what was really inside me opened me up to an entire universe. Not only did I gain insight into my personal emotional history, but I also started feeling the undercurrent of impermanence that is pervasive throughout all of reality. The learning accelerated to a new level that went beyond knowledge and started entering the realm of wisdom. This was a type of learning that superseded anything I had ever read about, a type of insight that could only be gained through direct experience. And the shifts in my internal life had an immediate effect on my external life, especially when it came to listening to the guidance of my intuition. In my new view, the world was elevated into higher definition— cultivating presence made everything around me look more vibrant and crisp. Self-awareness began to blossom and a greater sense of inner clarity helped me overcome the fear of being alone with my thoughts. My mind simply felt like it had new space where I could more intentionally choose the actions that felt most genuine and least harmful when tough situations would arise.

There was nothing perfect about this period, no great attainment, no sense of being fully healed or fully wise. I was not enlightened at all, but I did feel lighter. What I gained was an all-encompassing relationship with my humanity and a growing ability to accept the truth that rejecting change only makes life harder. Though my mind is no longer overburdened with tension and I have learned to dwell more in the present, I still feel that I am full of imperfection. The journey to grow in my healing and freedom continues. To this day, I feel like a student fortunate to learn from the wisdom that anyone can access when they observe reality within the framework of the body.

healing isn't about filling your life with pleasure
or never having a hard moment again
it's about being real
and facing what you feel
so that it doesn't accumulate in unhealthy ways
being with the down moments is better than
carrying unprocessed pain everywhere you go

Why Yung Pueblo and Why This Book

When I started meditating, two things became pristinely clear—that deep healing is possible and that humanity as a whole is young. When I felt plagued by sadness and anxiety, I could not imagine that such a heaviness could one day become lighter and manageable in a healthy way. As I progressed in my first year of moving in a healthier direction, and as I later started my meditation journey, it shocked me that I could actually feel better. This new sense of well-being wasn't me repressing my emotions or some sort of delusion. Instead, in a concrete and observable way, the root of my mental discontent was truly being alleviated. At a fundamental level, a real shift was taking place. While everyone heals differently because each of our emotional histories is unique, it became clear to me that healing is open and available to anyone who seeks it. Healing yourself is possible through letting go of the past and connecting with the present, all so you can expand your future. And healing progresses quickly when you find the practices that connect well with the conditioning your mind has developed over time.

As I continued learning through meditation, another idea that kept returning was that humanity has not yet matured. The basic things we are taught and start practicing as children—to clean up after ourselves, to tell the truth, to treat each other fairly, to share, to be kind to one another, not to harm each other—have not yet been successfully applied at the level of society. But these principles do show us a path to supporting the health and harmony of all people. In this century, in particular, it feels like we are in a special moment in human history, poised to face our great challenges and to come to terms with much of the harm that we directly and indirectly cause each other. This moment is an opening to grow deeply in our maturity so that we may build a world that is no longer structurally harmful but is structurally compassionate.

These two ideas converge in the name *yung pueblo*, which literally means "young people." This pseudonym reflects a social commentary that points to humanity's coming growth and maturation. The name signals a time when we will collectively transition from being ruled by shortsightedness and self-centeredness to having an elevated appreciation of our interconnectedness, which normalizes treating each other with a new and considerate gentleness. The evolution of the way humanity thinks and acts is spurred on by many factors. But one major factor stands out: the healing of the individual. All people do not need to be perfectly healed for us to live in a peaceful world, but as more and more people progress in their healing, this will create waves that can change the trajectory of human history. As more people heal themselves, our actions will become more intentional, our decisions will become more compassionate, our thinking will become clearer, and the future of the world will become brighter.

This book is meant as a bridge between the ideas of personal transformation and global transformation, to show that the two are deeply intertwined and function in support of each other. This book will hopefully serve not only as inspiration, but as a way to demystify personal healing and its benefits. While the primary focus is on the healing of the individual as you cross deeper thresholds and move from human habit to human nature, the journey concludes with an exploration of what is possible when compassion is scaled up from the interpersonal level to the structural level. *Lighter* aims to explore common understandings and experiences that people share when they go deep within themselves, regardless of the practice they are using, to navigate their inner world. Though human experience exists on a vast spectrum, there are some universals that can be highlighted to help us better understand ourselves and the world. I hope this book's message is one among the many forces that support the emergence of a world where harm is no longer systemic.

Meditation remains a huge part of my daily life but writing as "yung pueblo" has become a wonderful tool for me to process what I am understanding about healing. When I first started sharing my writing, I hoped that some of it would resonate with others, but I never imagined that so many people around the world would find solace and meaning in my work. I take the trust you give me seriously. And I will hold it gently.

Chapter 1

Self-Love

When I ask myself what I was addicted to, no particular drug or craving stands out as the one source that led me into darkness. After I stopped the serious drug abuse, I realized that I had been using a mixture of whatever could bring me temporary pleasure to cover up a void in myself that I did not have the courage to face. The void was never satiated or content. Any enjoyment I could experience or attention that people gave me was never enough. It felt like an endless vacuum that could take in the world, spit it out, and still have room to ask for more.

The shift finally came when I stopped throwing pleasure at the problem and started nourishing myself with nonjudgmental and honest attention. The refocusing of my energy into paying attention to all my changing emotions had an immediate effect. Paying attention eased my incessant craving for more pleasure and I stopped feeling so ragged and run-down.

I was not aware of the term *self-love* when my personal journey started, but I certainly used the practice as a critical stepping-stone. I would not have been able to move forward into a better life without this gentle and accepting attention that I started giving myself. Self-love was the missing link. It was the key to wholeness that I was unconsciously searching for. I discovered that the appreciation you seek from others will not hold the same rejuvenating power as the appreciation, attention, and kindness you can give yourself.

What Does *Self-Love* Mean?

Anything powerful and long-lasting requires a sturdy foundation. When a home is being constructed, all attention first goes to the foundation that will stabilize the structure. Once that foundation is firmly in place, you can go on to build, expand, and create something magnificent. The evolution of the individual works in a similar manner. Self-love is the first step that all inner and outer success is based on. Self-love gives your journey the energy and stability to stay on a clear trajectory. It is a profound commitment to self-discovery and to making your well-being a top priority.

Somewhere around 2014 or 2015, a big shift started happening culturally regarding the idea of self-love. In particular, I noticed that the word began entering the sphere of social media in a big way. I like to think of social media as a forum where humanity talks to itself, and at the time it felt as if we had collectively picked up the word *self-love* and started looking at it in different ways, turning it in all directions to get a better sense of its true meaning. Many individuals were asking themselves what *self-love* means to them, and at the same time I was going through my own process with the word. I wondered: Is self-love real? Is it needed? Is this something I can apply in my daily life? Is self-love different from self-centeredness? What is the relationship between self-love and healing yourself?

Initially, commercialization surrounded the idea, with mainstream media pushing the belief that you could buy yourself happiness and self-worth. But this is misleading because it confuses your needs with your cravings. The understanding that self-love means giving yourself all the things that you want, especially in the material sense, seems fine to a certain extent, but from the experience of many it is clear that material things can only go so far. Treating yourself to small gifts or going on rejuvenating trips can all fall under the umbrella of self-love, but self-love should not be confused with materialism. Material things cannot give you complete balance of mind and they cannot fundamentally heal your past. It is easy to go to extremes in trying to find solace in external or material things and end up further fueling the fire of craving that ultimately results in dissatisfaction. Thinking of self-love only as what you can buy or obtain does not activate its life-changing power.

Others understood self-love as putting yourself first at all costs. It makes sense that many would embrace this under-standing of self-love because too many of us live our lives for others and fall into cycles of people-pleasing without taking the time to properly take care of ourselves. However, we run the risk of falling into the trap of ego if we only think of ourselves. Putting ourselves first in all situations can quickly become another type of extreme that disregards the welfare of others and pushes us to become more and more self-centered. If your ego is growing, then your mind is full of agitation and will have great difficulty seeing reality clearly. If self-love is supposed to help our lives, then this must not be the right direction.

The understanding of self-love that makes the most sense to me is much more internal. It is the way you relate to yourself with compassion, honesty, and openness. It is meeting every part of yourself with unconditional acceptance, from the parts that you find easy to love, to the rough and imperfect parts that you try to hide from. Self-love begins with acceptance, but it does not stop there. Real self-love is a total embrace of all that you are while simultaneously ac-knowledging that you have room to grow and much to let go of. Real self-love is a tricky concept that requires a sense of balance to be able to use its transformative power—it is nourishing yourself deeply without becoming self-centered or egotistical. It is no longer seeing yourself as less than oth-ers, but at the same time maintaining the humility not to see yourself as better than others. The greatest benefits of self-love come from the positive interactions between you and yourself. Self-love is not only a mindset but a set of actions.

Taken to its highest form, self-love is an energy we use to evolve. Ultimately, I define *self-love* as "doing what you need to do to know and heal yourself."

True self-love is multifaceted and includes radical honesty, positive habit building, and unconditional self-acceptance. These three pillars work internally and externally to generate and support an enduring sense of self-love.

everywhere there was
once a lie inside of you
there is now truth
a truth that enhances
the connection between
you and yourself

Radical Honesty

Radical honesty, a form of authenticity that begins inside you, is a warm recognition that you gently apply to your conscious life. This view of radical honesty is not about telling everyone what you think. Instead, it is the root from which self-awareness grows. Thoughts and emotions that were once discarded or ignored are now embraced. Where you once felt the urge to run away, you now challenge yourself to face whatever is there. More than anything, any lie that you formerly told yourself is examined so that the truth may come forward. The key to radical honesty is that this is not about you and other people, but about how you relate to yourself in all situations, whether you are alone or with others.

Radical honesty is not about punishing yourself or harsh self-talk. Rather, it is about calmly being in constant contact with your truth. Practicing this balance is critical. In the beginning, radical honesty may feel hard to manage, but it is truly a long-term project. If you want to see great results, you need to wholeheartedly commit to the process, especially when it gets difficult, so you can reject the temptation to fall back into unconsciously motivated behavior.

If you continue to tread down the path of lies, fear and its two primary manifestations—anxiety and anger—will continue to grow. First, you fear truth and then you lie to be rid of your fear, unwittingly falling into a loop where you actually continue empowering your fear because every lie breeds further anxiety. The only way to put an end to the burning fire of fear is by thoroughly extinguishing it with truth. *Dishonesty is the fear of truth.*

Dishonesty with yourself creates distance. The more lies you build up over time, the more you become a stranger to yourself. When you cannot accept your own truth, you are moving in the opposite direction of self-awareness. When lies suffuse your mind, life becomes opaque and the right actions you need to take to ease your inner tension become difficult to decipher. The lies you tell yourself will also manifest as a lack of depth in your relationships. A deep connection with another being is not possible if you are deeply disconnected from yourself.

As you practice radical honesty, this distance decreases and your mind starts to become calmer. *Telling yourself the truth is the beginning of inner harmony.* This harmony immediately makes your relationships more vibrant. In examining your past and uncovering the truth that you previously refused to own, you actually make the power of your honesty stronger. This higher degree of presence allows your self-awareness to flourish. Eventually, your radical honesty matures to the point where it becomes non-negotiable—you carry it wherever you go and in every situation it becomes an asset that informs your decisions.

Where you once coaxed yourself into thinking nothing was wrong, you now admit to yourself that turbulence or hurt was actually there. Where you once forced yourself into thinking you liked something, you admit that you did find it disagreeable. Where you once denied old pain, you admit that there is a wound within you that needs tending.

Self-love is an invitation to our inner world. When we turn our attention inward, we come across the entirety of our conditioning. *Radical honesty is not just observing what you find—it also requires us to approach ourselves with curiosity.* Engaging ourselves through the medium of curiosity will take the old energy that we formerly used to run away from ourselves and give it a new purpose that helps us go deeper into our own truth. When we come across something difficult (for example, realizing that there is unresolved trauma regarding your relationship with your parent), we do not recoil in negativity, but instead ponder how it came to be and do our best to find its roots.

Curiosity is especially useful when intense emotions arise. When we encounter sadness, for instance, we can ask ourselves where it is coming from. When we find a hardened pattern, we can ask ourselves how it came to be. Was it a tactic of survival? Did it emerge from fear? Where is this sadness coming from? When did this pattern start forming? What triggers this pattern and how is this behavior affecting my life?

Curiosity can also help us trace a clear trajectory to our transformation. As we change and shed old layers, we will have to get to know ourselves again and again by periodically asking ourselves: What are my real aspirations? What has society encoded inside my mind that is not really mine to carry? Who do I really want to spend time with? How can I better align my actions to support my new evolution?

Radical honesty, reinforced by an inward curiosity, can help streamline our transformation. This momentum of honesty and a growing understanding of ourselves can become a source of power, helping us overcome old barriers and release baggage that we never intended to carry.

Positive Habit Building

Radical honesty leads to positive habit building. When we come to terms with the behaviors we have developed over time that limit our happiness and well-being, we realize that we need to intentionally build new habits. When we are honest with ourselves about what is not serving us, we can redirect our energy.

When I started practicing radical honesty, one of the first things I came to terms with was how I had been lying to myself about the state of my health. I was incredibly unhealthy. The smallest things would trigger my heart to fall out of rhythm. My lungs were exhausted and weak, and my eating habits were always making me feel depleted. I knew that if I wanted to turn my life around, I had to start here. Even though it was tremendously difficult, I broke through the barrier of stagnant patterns by going outside to jog and by adding more nutritious food to my normal diet. To be honest, the changes hurt at first. My body had not felt the strain of exercise in years, and my mind struggled because my sense of taste was not immediately pleased with my new food choices. Even so, it was one of those moments where I simply had to put my foot down. I was determined to live in a new way, so I had to face the discomfort that sometimes comes with personal transformation.

Positive habit building is a long-term game and the greatest results are not immediate—they come after you have doubled down on consistency. Understanding that you are building something great will help ease the craving for fast results. As the author James Clear put it so succinctly in his book *Atomic Habits*, "Every action you take is a vote for the type of person you wish to become. No single instance will transform your beliefs, but as the votes build up, so does the evidence of your new identity."

In my experience, trying to change everything at once does not work. Rather, focus on a few key changes. Continue pressing forward until what you wish to change no longer feels like a struggle, but a natural part of you. This is when you will know you have been successful.

Overhauling your entire life and turning everything upside down will divide your energy in too many directions. Instead, choose a focused strategy. Build a needed habit until it becomes firmly ingrained in your mind and body, then you can more easily stretch into new areas. The positive habit that you have spent so much time cultivating will not disappear when you switch your attention because you made sure to give it the time it needed to become a vital pillar in your life. When you have fully internalized a new habit, you feel less tension in doing it. The repetition of the habit no longer feels like serious work. Instead, it is more like an effortless routine that you might even enjoy. When I started meditating daily, it felt like a huge task I had to accomplish each day, but as I maintained my effort it became a part of my life that I now cannot imagine skipping.

When you allow your self-love to inform your decisions, it will challenge you to raise the standard you have for yourself. Self-love is not an overwhelming sense of positivity, it is the frank advice you need to give yourself so you can truly flourish. If you focus on repeating wholesome behaviors that nurture your being from the inside out, you will decrease the amount of inner struggle you used to feel daily.

Self-Acceptance

Self-love is a vehicle we use to travel through our own inner universe. What makes this journey productive is the self-acceptance we apply along the way. When we become open to self-discovery, our inner world will open up to us. Our history, which was once in the dark, will reveal itself under the light of self-awareness. The deep self-love that can make profound changes in our lives will turn us into explorers who bravely move inward to deepen our understanding of what makes us who we are. Without self-acceptance, any tough thing we come across would quickly stall or end our journey or have us running back to known territory. But when we understand that we are bound to come across difficult things and come prepared to meet ourselves with self-acceptance, we are more likely to embrace the hard parts of our conditioning and continue delving deeper into our emotional history.

To be clear, self-acceptance does not mean complacency. It just means that instead of rejecting or fighting whatever comes up, we acknowledge it for what it is and if there is a need to take action, we do so skillfully. What makes self-love powerful is that it is not just a way of seeing ourselves, but a series of actions that continuously align us with a greater vision of who we are growing into.

As we practice self-love, there will certainly be things we need to openly deal with and rectify, but feeling hate toward what we want to change will only cloud our minds and make our actions less effective. Self-acceptance is a deep embrace of reality, letting go of punishing ourselves for the past, and the foundation that balances all the other tools we use for personal transformation. When our self-love becomes active, transformation is immediately set in motion. No transformation carries an unbreakable upward trajectory—we are bound to stumble, to momentarily regress to old habits, to move a few steps back before taking a life-changing leap forward, or to experience moments when we simply need a break. In our personal journey, every moment will not be a victory. Especially during tough times, when inner turmoil arises, it does not help to have a strong aversion to our own tension—that will only make the heaviness we already feel worse. The best way to be prepared for the long journey is to move through the ups and downs with self-acceptance.

Self-Love Is a Gateway

Self-love helps us build internal cohesion so that we are no longer far away from ourselves. The more we come in contact with our truth and learn to embrace it with full acceptance, the more we are able to find greater personal harmony. Building this self-awareness opens up a gateway where we not only learn to love ourselves better, but we start to have a deeper sense of love for the people in our lives. At its highest levels, self-love continues expanding, ultimately becoming an opening to loving all beings unconditionally.

When you deeply get to know yourself through the energy of self-love, you start to learn about the human condition, and how your own heavy emotions and traumas have shaped your behavior and reactions over time. As you become less of a mystery to yourself, you can start to look at other people with a greater sense of clarity and compassion.

Though all human beings have very different histories, we all live through the same spectrum of emotions. Our minds may hold different contents, but their structure is relatively similar. For example, we all have a hard time remaining in the present. During difficult moments, our past will reemerge to try to help us make sense of a new experience by matching it to our past, but that then often activates old reactive patterns. Additionally, all of us at some time experience fear, greed, jealousy, anger, and other emotions that thicken our conditioning.

When we take a good look at the makeup of our own mind, we start to gain a deeper sense of compassion for others, because we have seen our own struggles and have begun the process of overcoming them. We can then more easily acknowledge and express love for others as they pass through difficult moments.

This growing sense of understanding ignites a deeper peace in our mind when we see loved ones struggle or even when we are dealing with a challenging person. As the spiritual leader Thich Nhat Hanh once wrote, "Understanding is the ground of love." After spending some time practicing self-acceptance and deepening my inner curiosity, I found that inner struggle is one of the great causes of outer conflict. It can be seen in moments when someone is tense and that tension narrows their ability to be patient with someone else, causing them to retort with angry words. It comes out in moments when we don't realize how childhood trauma contributes to unproductive patterns in our intimate relationships as adults. Whenever your ability to see yourself increases, so, too, does the patience you have with the people around you.

As we make progress in our personal transformation and as our self-love takes on a new level of maturity, our love for others will continue to expand. It takes the form of a wise and balanced love, meaning that we feel for others without forgetting about ourselves. A love where we understand how essential it is to treat ourselves well so we can show up for others in an effective way.

When taken to its highest level, self-love becomes the foundation that allows us to feel and express unconditional love. Without self-love, all other forms of love will remain superficial. An individual who is completely free does not harbor any ill will in their heart or mind. Their being will radiate love for all beings, whether or not they have encountered them in person. This is not just a quiet love felt within oneself, but a love that can take action whenever necessary. Real love is flexible—like water, it can sit in stillness or flow with tremendous power.

The Bridge Between Self-Love and Healing

As I activated my self-love, I developed a clearer picture of my mind and what it carried. I could feel the sadness that had accumulated over time, the anxiety that would spike whenever things became difficult, and the tension whenever

I felt that I was not getting what I craved. All these dense patterns would have remained hidden had it not been for self-love.

Radical honesty, positive habit building, and self-acceptance were giving me real results. But once I started recognizing the struggle that my mind was constantly rolling in, I realized that this was not going to be a short adventure with a quick fix. If I wanted to get to the root of my problems and really address the deepest layers of my mind, I realized that I had to wholeheartedly commit to a long journey of healing. Self-love gently walked me inward, introduced me to myself, and showed me that I not only needed to double down on the nourishing behavior that I was focusing on, but I had to gather my bravery and dig deeper so I could start the process of healing.

Self-love and healing are deeply intertwined, and if you take one of them seriously, the other will be immediately activated. They rise and fall together. Similarly, if the two are flourishing, a profound transformation is bound to take place.

Reflection

At the end of each chapter I have included questions that I hope will encourage personal reflection and vulnerability for the sake of self-discovery. They can be taken as journal prompts for you to go deep into processing parts of yourself or as something you can keep in the back of your mind and think back on as you move through your day. These are also questions that can be explored in a safe setting with a friend or loved one.

What does self-love look like for you right now? How do you want your self-love to evolve, and what do you want it to feel like a year from now?

What part of yourself do you have trouble accepting? Is this a critical part of your story?

What positive habits are you working on developing? Is there a way to use boundaries to support yourself in the cultivation of the new you?

Has building your self-love helped you have more compassion for others? Has understanding yourself helped you see them more clearly?

What is your relationship to honesty these days? Can you be honest with yourself when your mind is full of tension?

How has a lack of self-love affected your relationships in the past?

Chapter 2

Healing

When I think about the situations that have most left an impact on my mind, the continuous struggle of poverty my family went through stands out the most. Growing up as a poor immigrant in the United States was incredibly challenging, and my personal trauma is deeply tied to that experience. I was fortunate to have a father and mother who loved each other dearly and treated me and my siblings incredibly well, but they had little to no opportunity for upward mobility because they were not college educated and did not speak fluent English. My parents took a great risk moving to the United States; they knew their lives would be hard, but they also knew their children would have opportunities that were not available in Ecuador. Poverty pushed hard against the safety of the home my parents were trying to create for us. They endured tremendous stress trying to pay bills and to make sure we had proper meals. This stress and the reality that they could not come up with a long-term plan for our economic advancement permeated the entire family. Our immediate needs were so pressing that at times even the strong love my parents had for each other was strained by the immense pressure that survival placed on us as a family.

As a child, I would wonder if my parents were right for each other because they were often arguing. Now, as an adult, I can see that there was no lack of love between them. What was happening was a structural problem: Having very little money filled their minds with tension and they often projected that tension onto each other. Their relationship today is quite different—their love for each other is clear and there is so much harmony between them—but part of the reason they can breathe easily now is that my brother, my sister, and I are all grown up, we take care of ourselves now, and we give them financial support. Their fights were situational, not because they were mismatched.

Over the years, the stress that suffused my family and the struggle I saw my parents go through to make ends meet became embedded in my mind. I especially remember the constant scramble to pay the rent every month for our small apartment. Most months, I would hear my parents argue about this, their voices full of stress and exhaustion as they tried to figure out their next move. As a child, I would wonder if this problem would ever end or if it would become worse. I remember this strong feeling of insecurity running through my body that made me feel like the floor could cave in at any moment. I remember feeling sadness for my parents and wishing that I could help them in some way. There was also a combination of anger and shame. Anger for the fact that something like poverty even existed and shame for the fact that I knew we were barely getting by each week. It felt unfair that my family had to struggle so much to simply exist. All of this manifested quietly as anxiety and more deeply as a craving for more, which is common in all human beings. Fear found fertile ground in my mind, often creating visions of the worst outcomes possible. Our mode of survival did not help the inclination toward sadness that I've had for as long as I can remember.

My constant craving for more, plus the feeling of ever-present insecurity and an enduring sense of sadness, only became worse as I entered my teen years and then became a young adult in college. Scarcity made me more attached—I would cling to the few things that I would get and crave so much of what I could not afford. I had to heal.

If you were to honestly examine your own life and mind, you would also likely find something specific from your past that you could try to heal. At the very least, this reflection would help you see that, yes, you could be happier—and that there is room to increase your inner peace and mental clarity. All human beings carry tension in the mind that inhibits them from living their best life. But, fortunately, the tension that accumulates within us can also be released. *Healing is when you intentionally decrease the tension you carry in your mind.*

The human mind is commonly full of stress and anxiety. It does not do a good job focusing on the present moment and it is full of attachments that get in the way of living peacefully and making effective decisions. Honoring the fact that our ups and downs have affected us deeply opens us up to learning how to live in a better way.

Left to its old patterns, our mind will continue its reactivity and keep us functioning on autopilot. What the mind knows best is repetition, which normally keeps us in a state of survival mode that defaults into blind behavior, especially when difficult situations arise. Even when an emotion is hard on the body, like stress or anxiety, we will continue repeating it if it is a way we have reacted in the past. Each reaction will even go as far as to slowly mold our perception, to the point where everything we perceive is first filtered through a thick layer of old conditioning, combined with our current emotions. Since our perception is being driven by our past and our emotions, it will inhibit our ability to recognize reality as it is. The mind will not do what is good for it unless we intentionally train it to do so.

Healing begins with the willingness to become an explorer, to enter the vast inner forest that exists within your being, using your awareness as the light that shows you the way. It is a journey that is challenging and sometimes filled with difficulty, because you will undoubtedly come across shadows and parts of yourself that may be hard to fully embrace with self-acceptance. But this is a challenge that can bring unparalleled rewards. When you are able to see yourself clearly, you awaken your true inner power. There is a universe inside each one of us that is untapped and largely undiscovered, but most people walk the earth unaware that they are not seeing with their eyes. Instead, they are seeing with their emotions, and often these emotions are just the echoes of their past hurts. Many fall into cycles of projection where they are taking their inner roughness and spewing it out into the world.

Deep healing and emotional maturity begin when you turn your attention inward. The ability to see yourself as you move through the ups and downs of life, without running away or suppressing your feelings, enhances your understanding of yourself. Feel your emotions as they come and go. Come to terms with your past and notice the way it shows up in your present. Watch your mind as it processes difficult situations. Take note of behavior patterns that show up repeatedly in your life. Examine your inner narrative and how your own thinking affects your emotions. Paying close attention to all these mental movements opens the door to the type of learning that can transform your life. But none of these qualities of the mind occur on their own. They need to be intentionally activated and consistently cultivated to become strong enough to alter our mental health and shift us from surviving to thriving.

Building your self-awareness increases the agility of your mind. When you make time to be present in your own mind, it becomes possible to slow things down when difficult situations arise. Rather than falling back into blind reactions that are rooted in your past, you can intentionally *lean into pausing* and give yourself a moment to take a look at what is actually happening. This ability to pause is not easy and it takes time to build this quality of the mind, but the results of this practice are immense. Giving yourself time to witness reality without immediately reacting is a sign of progress in your healing. Now that you can see yourself and give yourself more time to process what is happening, you can more easily behave in ways that align with your goals and honor your authenticity. Finding the balance where you can be honest about what you are feeling and not allow a temporary emotion to take total control of your actions can help you better handle the unexpected changes of life.

Oftentimes, people want to improve their lives but they end up focusing on the things around them instead of what is happening within them. Changing your location as a way to start a new life can be helpful, but if you never address your mindset, old patterns ingrained in your mind can re-create the situations you were trying to remove yourself from. People will reassess their goals and have an idea of the particular life they want to manifest, but things don't simply fall into place that easily. A vision remains a vision until action is applied to it. There is a common trope that makes its rounds on the internet—"What is for you will come to you"—but life is never that simple. The missing piece of that puzzle is that life will continue to be difficult and you will block yourself from enjoying good things if you never deal with the heaviness of your mind and the fear that clutters your heart. The things that are for you will come to you much more easily when you are deeply aligned with your truth and pursuing your growth. The shape of your internal dynamic always influences what will come your way. Your inner blocks, meaning the parts of your conditioning that you do not realize are resisting your freedom, have a way of pushing things away from you until they are unbound. If your mind is full of anger and tension, peace simply won't be possible and the things that do come your way won't aid in your quest for happiness. Similar vibrations tend to attract each other, and if we don't align ourselves with peace, then harmony will have a hard time coming into our lives. Healing will not only improve your life, but it will open the door for good things to come to you because the quality of your mind determines the quality of your life.

The other key factor that should not be overlooked is that your effort is critical. It is one thing to know what you want, but another is following through on your dream by making a plan and acting on it. Leaving things to the whim of hope or simply waiting for things to come to you is a passive approach to life that does not yield great results. A big part of healing yourself effectively is taking responsibility for your patterns. Even though the trauma or hurt you went through, which fueled these patterns, was not your fault—especially if you were a child when it happened—the healing of these patterns can only be done by you. People can certainly help you, but it is your intention and effort that will help you evolve past the hurt you carry. If there is one thing to focus on for improving your life, your healing should be it. If you want to build a better life, you have to concentrate on what impacts you the most, and without a doubt that is the relationship between you and your mind. If you get deep into your healing, the effort that you then apply to achieving your aspirations and dreams will be much more efficient and produce results more quickly. A healed mind is incredibly powerful.

One of our strongest tendencies is to point to the source of our problem as if it were outside of us. Our ego likes to place blame outside ourselves, and often that blame falls on those closest to us. One day Sara, my wife, came into the kitchen where I was working and with a smile on her face began telling me how she had been arguing with me in her head for the last few hours. She had a lot of anger come up that day that was not triggered by anything in particular. Even so, her mind kept trying to figure out how this anger could be my fault. Her mind went back further and further in time to find a suitable reason, but in recognizing this pattern, she regained her power and the anger eventually subsided. We ended up sharing a good laugh as she described how her mind was jumping through hoops as it tried to reject any responsibility for its own tension. Her honesty also helped me see how I would fall into that same pattern in my own mind—the tension that would arise in me would often try to build a reason that would make it her fault when it actually had nothing to do with her.

Granted, there will be times when someone will do something to us that clearly does trigger anger, but many times this will not be the case. Whenever anger or another heavy emotion appears in the theater of your mind, it will start looking for more fuel, even if it has to bend logic to do so. This is something that will come up again and again, even as you make progress in your healing. A commitment to patiently reminding yourself that you are the maker of your destiny will help you reassert yourself as the one who is in charge of your mental state.

You will be surprised at how powerful it is simply to be aware of what's happening in your mind and then use your intention to pull yourself back in the right direction. We tend to want to overcomplicate things. But the simple act of redirecting where your mental energy is going, even if you have to do so multiple times, will help you build the habits and sense of gratitude you need to be happier. This is why self-awareness is so critical. When you can see the way your mind is moving, you can then use your intention to course-correct as necessary. Now this doesn't mean suppressing anything. We need to accept the idea that the mind is expansive—you can hold space for multiple versions of yourself. You can honor the feelings brought on by your past that keep trying to come up, or a heavy emotion that seeks your attention, without letting any of this heaviness take over your mind. It is possible to honor where you are and where you want to be by feeling the reality of the heaviness but not giving it power over your actions. This is one of the key mental shifts that I hope this book gives you—the art of being real and staying true. *Be real by accepting what you are feeling and stay true by maintaining your growth mission even when things get hard. The key is that you can feel it without becoming it.*

maturity is when you can finally ride
the ups and downs of life
without getting tossed around by them
you don't expect everything to be perfect
you know change is a constant
you don't judge yourself when times get hard
you live in gratitude
you enjoy the good when it is here

The problem is that most people want an easier answer, a quick fix, but that is not how healing works. Patterns are built over decades, and reactions that have accumulated over long spans of time gather deep in the subconscious and harden like concrete. Fortunately, your will and intention are mighty tools. Healing can certainly happen in shorter spans of time than decades, but, even so, it will take real effort to break your old ways. Quick fixes normally provide superficial results. If you aren't ready to dig deep in your emotional trenches and face the tough truths that have been waiting for you in the shadows, then this work will be harder than it already is. The toughest part of healing is staying inspired so you can keep plugging away at building the new you, thought by thought, action by action, step by step. All these seemingly small movements eventually add up to a total transformation. People who heal themselves are lions, heroes with exceptional bravery—and I say this not to discourage you, but to make it clear that this journey is not fast, not easy. This is a really long commitment. There can be no time limit set. You have to love yourself to change yourself, and loving yourself does not take days off. But through acceptance, patience, and effort, you can support the person you are becoming.

Healing is not about perfection; it is about no longer living unconsciously. We can spend years constantly giving our power away by never taking responsibility for what is happening in our own minds. *Healing is about illuminating your mind with your own awareness, turning on the light within so brightly that your old patterns no longer have anywhere to hide.* Finally being able to see yourself clearly will help you reclaim the fullness of your power. Change is not possible if you cannot see what needs to be changed. The power of your attention is grand and immeasurable. When you bring that attention inward, it will help you remove all the blocks that stood in the way of your building a great mind and thus a great life.

Emotional History

Healing is needed because everything we feel leaves a mark on the mind, and it all accumulates in our conditioning: our family dynamics, what we learned in school, our relationships with friends and partners, the views society imposes on us throughout our lives, our own relationship with ourselves, and any other experience or bit of information that passes through our being. All this comes together to create the totality of our conditioning. Our conditioning does not sit quietly—it permeates how we perceive ourselves, those we interact with, and the world. Our conditioning does more than impact our perception, it goes even further and molds the way we behave. When we talk about healing, and what we are actually healing from, we mean the heavy conditioning that is overloading the mind and slowing us down from living authentically. Our conditioning is literally the past that we carry with us wherever we go.

The conscious mind is sometimes able to forget, but the subconscious mind accumulates every reaction from the past. These reactions harden over time and develop into specific behavior patterns that arise when the mind is reminded of a past situation. Have you ever felt impatient when you needed to wait in line, or anger rising when you were stuck in traffic? When you already have a lot on your plate and someone adds another to-do item that is high priority, do stress and anxiety start to creep in? When someone is rude or condescending, do you react defensively? These are just a few examples of common reaction patterns. How intensely we feel these reactive patterns is directly related to how many times we have reacted like this in the past. Healing is processing and unloading all the programming from the past that hinders our ability to live freely in the present.

Healing does not erase the past, and the point of healing is not to forget what has happened. Old memories from hard moments may come up even after deep healing has taken place, but what shifts is how we react to them when they arise. *If the intensity of the reaction is decreasing, then real progress is being made.* This has nothing to do with suppressing the reaction; it is just a measure of what is actually happening in the mind. It is possible to feel your truth without getting consumed by it or letting it control your behavior.

One of the most dominant parts of our conditioning is our personal emotional history, the lingering feelings that have stayed with us that relate specifically to the strong emotions we have felt throughout our lives. Developing an understanding of what we have personally gone through and how these challenges manifest in our emotional and behavioral patterns helps us unlock the rigidity of our reactions. Instead of being trapped in a cycle that repeats the past, we can break the cycle, make different decisions, and feel things other than our most prominent defensive emotions. Our emotional history can sometimes be so dense that it limits our capacity to change our behavior to the point that it keeps us in a state of mere survival. But no emotional baggage from the past is beyond healing.

Finding My Patterns

After hitting my rock bottom and spending a whole year practicing the three aspects of self-love—radical honesty, positive habit building, and self-acceptance—I had seen significant results, but my intuition was calling me to go deeper.

During that same time, one of my best friends from college, Sam, had been spending some time traveling through India. While he was there, a family that he was staying with told him about a silent ten-day meditation course that sparked his curiosity, and he tried it not long afterward. He went in looking for a new experience and unexpectedly found something much greater: He found his path.

After the course, he sent a long email to me and three other close friends. His message was all about love, compassion, and goodwill. I remember feeling shocked, as our friendship up until that point had never covered such topics. In fact, I had never heard him talk like this. I always thought of him as a trusted friend, but our previous conversations never entered into spaces of vulnerability. I could tell he was sharing his truth with us and that those ten days had ignited a serious transformation in him. His note came at a time when I was new to healing, but committed to the journey. While I had only meditated for about twenty minutes once in my life, after hearing about how powerful an experience he had, my intuition told me right away that this was something I needed to try. I signed up for a course that teaches the same technique here in the United States. Whatever he had gotten, I needed some of that, too.

During July 2012, I did my first Vipassana meditation course. This type of meditation dates back to the Buddha's original teaching, but this modern interpretation of Vipassana comes to us from S. N. Goenka, a Burmese man of Indian descent who learned from his teacher Sayagyi U Ba Khin. In 1969 Goenka started teaching in India, and over time Vipassana spread across the world. To this day, I think of S. N. Goenka as my teacher, though he passed away in 2013 before I had a chance to meet him in person.

My first meditation course was incredibly difficult. I struggled all the way through as my old conditioning tried very hard to reject the practice. All I could think about was how I wanted to leave. A few days into the course I remember looking at the guy who gave me a ride to the retreat, wondering if he wanted to leave, too, but he seemed committed to staying. This was before Uber and Lyft were popular, so I had no way to get home. The retreat was in a small town in the state of Washington and I was a long ride away from anyone I knew. Today, I am so grateful that there was no easy way for me to get home and that I stayed in the course. Around the seventh day, I finally settled down, stopped thinking about escaping, and started putting more effort into meditating. When the retreat was over, I knew that I had come across something special that really fit the type of deep healing I was looking for. I undeniably felt better than I ever had in my life. My mind felt lighter and more open, my emotions did not feel clogged up anymore, and it was easier for me to appreciate life and enjoy each moment. In no way was I totally healed, but I glimpsed that if I kept practicing I would continue to get deep and life-changing results.

I felt such a drastic shift in my mind after the first course that I signed up to do another in September 2012. I knew that I was getting so much from the technique, but I didn't quite understand how it worked and I wanted to learn how to practice better. Quickly it became clear that the investment healing requires is your own effort and time. The more you put into it, the greater the results. I got into a good routine of doing a few courses a year. It was a big time commitment, but I knew my healing had to come first. I needed to make my well-being a top priority and directly deal with all the unhealthy patterns I had built up over my lifetime.

What felt truly shocking was that real healing was possible. While I was growing up, I had unknowingly adopted the idea that the mental burdens you carry will be yours to carry forever. I did not understand how malleable the mind is and how intentional, introspective action can alleviate personal suffering. At first, I would question if these changes were real, if my mind did feel lighter. I wanted to make sure I wasn't suppressing anything. But the changes were real: When things would get really hard, I did not run back to hard drugs and the ups and downs of life did not feel as extreme. More evidence of genuine change showed up in how I treated others. In the past it was easy to default into selfishness—a long history of scarcity can make people self-centered—but increasingly my mind felt this new abundance of love and compassion for others that felt totally new. It was active and present even during challenging moments.

Around 2015, I had grown and healed to a place where I finally had the energy to bring meditation into my daily life. I continue meditating in this same style and tradition today. I still find it hard to quantify the amount of healing that meditation ignited, but what is clear is that when the challenges of life appear, I no longer feel a need to run away or suppress tough emotions. Meditating taught me to focus on building equanimity (balance of mind, the ability to observe without craving or aversion), instead of allowing the mind's reactions to roll on endlessly. This unbinding process is helping purify what has been accumulating in my subconscious. I can now observe what is true within my mind and body with a new calmness, rather than just reacting and multiplying tension. My mind does not feel perfect or fully wise, and the walk to total liberation continues, but I do have a clear path that makes me feel that the steps forward I have taken are real and substantial. Who I was before—when my mind was riddled with pain, anxiety, and insecurity— is long gone. I still feel tough emotions, but with nowhere near the same intensity as before. Though the journey continues, the tension in my mind has decreased and I am able to show up in my life and the lives of loved ones in a more effective way. And that feels like a true victory.

your immediate reaction
does not tell you who you are
it is how you decide to respond after the reaction
that gives you real insight
into how much you have grown
your first reaction is your past
your intentional response is your present

More than Childhood

Since each individual has their own unique prism of conditioning, why we seek healing is unique to our own journey. Some of the major things that appear as challenges in life may include childhood pain and trauma, hurt that occurs after childhood, being unaware, patterns that have hardened over time, blind reactions, and having no boundaries. A lot of our most dense conditioning is accumulated during childhood, which has a major impact on our personality and patterns, but our conditioning never stops being molded. Every time we react and feel one heavy emotion or another, it leaves an imprint in the subconscious of the mind, which shifts our conditioning. Childhood has a massive impact, but so does any hurt you feel as you move through your life. All emotions are not only felt in the moment, every time we react to them, they set us up to feel them again and again in the future. Our character is never fully set in stone, as our subconscious is always moving, just like any other aspect of the universe. And it has the capability to let old patterns go or acquire new ones. The human mind remains malleable and mutable throughout its life span. Any time you react with intensity, it will leave a mark on your present and potentially on your future as well. As your subconscious shifts, whether it is continuing the long stream of simply accumulating more and more imprints or if it is doing the opposite and cleansing itself of what it contained, it will cause changes in your personality. A human being can never stay the same. At the core of what we truly are is change. Our power, and the reason that healing is even possible, lies in the fact that with intention we can give the natural flow of change within us a clear direction, as opposed to just unconsciously riding the ups and downs of life.

One of the biggest misconceptions is that our reactions are driven by what we think or by what is done to us by other people. On the surface, this may seem to be so because the mind moves so rapidly, but as the Buddha clarifies in his teaching and as S. N. Goenka also highlights in his ten-day courses, there is a subtler process happening that a heightened awareness will eventually be able to perceive. Specifically, the thoughts that arise in the mind simultaneously arise with sensations in the body. *Our reaction is not to what we think, but to what we feel.* If we think about something we like or if we hear, taste, feel, or see something that we perceive as pleasant, the body will feel pleasantness and we will react to that feeling with craving, wanting more and more of whatever we find agreeable, but which is inevitably impermanent. The same process occurs when we encounter something disagreeable and then we experience an unpleasant sensation in the body that we react to. The tension we feel in the mind is driven by the distaste we have for the unpleasant sensations that are happening in the body. The speed of these mental processes makes them largely invisible. We are very intellectual beings—

always thinking, speaking, processing, analyzing—but we fail to realize how big an effect feeling and the reaction to what we feel has on our stress and mental conditioning.

Other people can certainly do harmful things to us—I am not minimizing that reality. And when faced with potential harm to ourselves or others we should take strong, intentional action to prevent harm from being caused. However, it is valuable to understand that the process of perception and reaction to how we feel is happening within our own mind, as opposed to things outside of us determining our emotions. Being able to see the power our reaction has over our mood and the amount of tension we feel in the mind can show us how much suffering we have been causing ourselves. This realization also gives us hope for future healing because how we react is not set in stone. Healing means we get to live a more peaceful, less tense life, rather than dwelling on past hurt forever. If we recognize the root of our tension, we can start to address it in a way that meets us where we are.

Healing versus Liberation

A quick note on healing versus liberation. I write from the understandings I have developed through direct experience, but that experience would not have been possible if I had not taken the Buddha's teaching seriously. A lot of my understanding regarding attachments and reactions are within the context of what the Buddha taught and what I have observed through meditation. I went into meditation for the sake of transformation. Intuitively, I felt that meditating could help me heal the heaviness in my mind and put me on a path to a better life. That was definitely what I got by going on retreats, but, over time, the more nuanced aspects of the Buddha's teaching started becoming clearer, and the idea that full liberation was possible started making sense. I had already encountered the idea of collective liberation while working as a community organizer, so it felt natural to me that liberation could also have an internal and personal dynamic for the individual. In the teaching of Vipassana, the pervasiveness of dissatisfaction that humans feel is due to craving, but it's possible for all of us to fully eradicate craving and thus be fully liberated.

Healing and liberation travel alongside each other well because our mental pain is due to the severity of our knee-jerk and uncontrolled reactions. Real healing will help ease the intensity of those reactions. The path of liberation does this same work, but it also goes much further. If someone decides to walk the entirety of the path, they will eventually reach the complete end of suffering.

The focus of this book is healing, and it deals with the thresholds many of us cross as we deepen our healing work, whether we are doing so through some form of meditation, therapy, or other healing techniques that are making a positive impact in our lives. Healing is for everyone, whether or

HEALING

not we are spiritual, because we all know what it is like to
have a mind that feels too heavy and emotions that over-
whelm us. For me, personally, I knew that healing was what
I needed, but the method that best suited me ended up introducing me to a serious liberation path. It is a path that I
walk to this day and one that I plan on continuing to walk
because I have much ground to cover. Even though the path
I walk emerges from a particular tradition, there are similarities in the healing experience that become evident when
you turn your attention inward.

To Each Their Own

Meditation has been my avenue for healing, but it is not the
only way to heal. No modality has a monopoly on how to
heal. What is special about the time we live in is that there
are a vast number of introspective methods that are giving
people substantive results.

While we all move through similar spectrums of emotions and experience similar battles with attachments and
old patterns, we all have unique conditioning that sets us
apart from each other. No two people have traveled the
same journey, and we each have our own emotional history
that we have to traverse when we start our healing.

Since each individual has their own conditioning, how
one person heals is not how all people heal. This is one of
the tricky aspects of doing introspective work. You have to

find your own way by finding the right tool or technique for you. Luckily, you do not have to reinvent the wheel. Healing practices are abundant and becoming more accessible. What works for a friend of yours or a family member may not be the right approach for you. It is important to take note of what feels right to you as you start your own personal journey because what you are doing should click with your intuition. The key is to find something that is challenging but not overwhelming. You know you are in that sweet spot when you have the energy to process what comes up as you turn your attention to your emotional history. Some people have experienced such serious trauma that their conditioning will need a gentle approach when they start going inward, while others may be able to handle a more robust healing method right off the bat.

Real healing is a deconditioning process that helps you unravel the blocks, narratives, and inflexibility that create space between you and your happiness. Healing starts with knowing yourself and loving yourself. When you see and feel how much you carry, it becomes clear that it is time to start letting go.

Reflections

Are you in touch with your emotional history?

What parts of you need healing?

What are some of the major patterns that appear repeatedly in your life? What about the patterns that appear when things get tough?

How has your childhood affected your conditioning and your personality?

What hurt stands out that occurred after childhood, and in what ways has this reverberated through your life?

Do you see the connection between your past and the ways you impulsively react?

Chapter 3

Letting Go

In my own journey, my struggle with sadness would repeatedly come up. It was a common reaction to difficult situations and sometimes it would appear without a cause. When I was writing my first book, *Inward*, I would get randomly hit with a great amount of melancholy that would sometimes stretch for days. Writing a book felt like a massive task to accomplish and my mind would take that uneasiness and react to it with sadness. During that time, I was already meditating daily, so a lot of what I harbored inside myself was already coming up for me to face. The sadness was focused on my present feelings of inadequacy, but these heavy emotions were much older than that. When the healing begins, the strong emotions that surface are sometimes triggered by the present, but what you are feeling is actually from your past. Later on, I recognized that each time sadness was arising within me, my mind was just cleaning itself out. Sticking to meditating through that time helped me more efficiently process all that stagnant sadness that had been sitting in my subconscious since I was a child. Whether in daily life or while in meditation, it became something I had to face for years. The shift came gradually over time. When it would appear, I would feel its weight and offer it acceptance. Over time, its heaviness lifted. I still feel sadness occasionally, but not with the same overwhelming force as before.

let go more than once
let go when an old pattern
wants to drag you back into the past
let go when narratives
run wild in your mind
let go every time you try
to cause yourself extra trouble
there is healing in repetition
soon, peace will feel familiar

Letting go is essentially a profound acceptance of the present moment. To be able to accept what is, we have to relinquish our hold on how we wish things to be. The transformative process of letting go is a gradual journey. We have to slowly train ourselves to stop living in the past and set aside the emotional baggage we carry. Even as we heal our past, it will continue to show up as potential pathways that lead back to old behavior, but as we become more attuned to the present, we can shift our relationship to the options that keep popping up in our mind when difficult things happen. This doesn't mean suppressing or ignoring the past. The pull to behave in old ways weakens over time as we keep choosing to behave in new ways that honor the present more than the past. *How we focus our mental energy can determine the future of our life.*

Without realizing it, we tend to hold on to any tension that may arise instead of letting it go. One of the great struggles that comes with being human is that we find ourselves in a process of constant accumulation, deeply imprinting ways of behaving and feeling into our subconscious every time we react. Whether caused by a serious external situation that triggers the tension or an imaginary narrative that starts suffusing our mind, our immediate reaction is not to bring ourselves back to reality and use our mental energy to regain our balance. Instead, we get caught in a loop where we throw tension on top of the tension that is already there.

Most of our reactions are impulsive. When emotions

spark, we quickly jump into feeding them and making them stronger, without realizing that this behavior just reinforces how we will feel in the future when a similar situation arises. Over and over again, the mind will see the present through the lens of the past, keeping us in a state of repetition and slowing down our ability to behave and think in new ways.

Holding on is a survival tactic born out of fear and scarcity. Fear is the craving for safety. A mind that is dominated by fear is a mind that is still in survival mode. Even when there is relative calm in our external environment, a mind that lives in survival mode will adopt a defensive stance and will often explore imaginary scenarios of what could go wrong as a way to remain prepared. There is nothing wrong with being mindful of our safety, but all too easily this can devolve into an extreme, where our anxiety is always on high alert. Living through fear keeps us far away from peace.

Before we can truly understand how to let go, we need to understand what we are holding on to. Beyond the base level of remaining attached to the way we want things to be, there are also a number of misconceptions ingrained in our psyche that hold us back from being completely free. It's beneficial to look more deeply at a few common areas that cause us much inner struggle. When we know where we struggle, we have an opportunity to address and undo the blocks that get in our way.

The Trouble We Cause Ourselves

If you are open to experiencing a profound transformation, you need to come to terms with the fact that much of your struggle is self-imposed. How many times has your imagination disturbed a perfectly peaceful moment? How many times have your cravings blocked you from fully enjoying the abundance in front of you? How many times have you impatiently waited for a particular moment—and then, once you were there, your mind started fixating on what it was missing? There is always more to want. The mind has a strong pattern that bends it toward dissatisfaction. It will pick things apart without realizing that, in the process, it is undermining its own joy.

Owning your power also means owning the responsibility for your happiness and for your healing. By doing this, you will be able to manage the things that are actually within your control. It feels easier to live life constantly blaming other people for any tension you may feel in your mind, getting pushed around without clear direction, and constantly letting your present-day feelings be governed by the hard moments that happened in the past. But know that it feels so much better once you let go of being the victim and take responsibility for your life. While many of us have encountered serious trauma and some people have done us incredible harm, if we want to repair and heal the imprints that burden our subconscious and skew our perception, we need to embrace the hard work of becoming our own hero. There is no way around it. When it comes to you and the inner workings of your mind, no one has the power or authority to save you the way you can save yourself. All therapists, meditation teachers, counselors, and coaches can do is guide you to reclaim your own power. A guide is not a savior. A guide is simply the person who can show you how to walk the right path so that you can finally live without having to carry so many mental burdens.

Many of us believe that other people are causing all our internal stress and tension. And if they changed, the thought goes, our lives would be radically improved. We fail to recognize the trouble we cause ourselves. If the people around you changed, that would certainly be helpful, but that is not something you have control over, especially if the person around you is seriously harmful. You can't force them to change. In these situations it is best to lean on your own power and remove yourself from the harm that is coming your way. No matter what you may say to them, only they can make a change. And their change can only come from within. You can serve to inspire, but you cannot walk the path for anyone else.

Thinking that the sole source of your stress is external is an illusion, one that we all fall for until we turn our awareness inward and pay close attention to the way our mind moves. People can certainly do mean or harmful things to us, but the way we perceive and react to what is happening lies within our own mind. The intensity of our reaction sets the tone of our stress level: the bigger the reaction, the greater the stress. If our past has been full of stress, that can cause our stress reaction to become much more easily triggered. When that happens, seemingly small things can cause wildly disproportionate stress reactions.

The biggest improvement to your life will come from you changing yourself. Since the amount of stress you experience depends on the intensity of your reaction, the only solution that is within your control is changing yourself. Constantly pointing the finger at other people will never make your stress go away. Your only route to happiness is developing greater self-awareness, combined with more wisdom regarding the human condition. Part of letting go is recognizing that we are a function of our past. As a result, our emotional whims normally have great power over what we think, say, and do. Often, what other people do has very little to do with us and a lot to do with how they currently feel and the density of the emotional history they themselves carry.

Everything changes when you realize that the challenge itself isn't the toughest part—it is your reaction to the challenge that is filling your mind with tension and struggle. Before you can set yourself free, you first need to understand how you make things harder for yourself. Many of us do not realize how we get stuck in a reactive loop, always allowing external events to dictate how we feel, without fully accepting that our real power emerges from training our mind to observe. If you spent more time observing than reacting, you would start to notice how the absence of reaction also means the absence of tension. The absence of reaction is essentially a profound ability to let go. If you spent your whole life reacting, don't expect your ability to observe to become perfectly honed overnight. It takes time and intention to break a habit that has been repeated countless times.

Letting go of the passive belief that you don't have power over your mental situation is critical. The greatest lever that affects your mood is reaction. Reaction to not feeling good makes you feel worse. Reaction to disliking something pushes you into anger. Reaction creates the fire of a tumultuous mind and then continuously feeds that fire, making it hotter and all-encompassing. When you understand how much of your inner troubles are based on uncontrolled reactions, you start to see how managing your reactions can help you improve your life. Managing reactions does not mean suppressing emotions. Being thoroughly honest with yourself means embracing all your emotions without rejecting those that are harder to feel. Managing your reactions does ask you to develop a more subtle understanding of what happens in your mind when things get tough.

Normally, when our emotions come up, we allow them to overcome us, and we then *become* them. We let the intense emotion take the reins and govern our perception and behavior. Managing our reactions means being aware when a tough emotion has appeared and understanding that even if we have an initial reaction, we do not need to keep feeding that reaction. We can honor the fact that the emotion is there without fully becoming it. Instead of throwing more fire onto it, we focus on observing it and remind ourselves that this emotion will change, eventually, as all things do. *The biggest asset to personal transformation is awareness.*

Once you turn your attention inward, you will start to see more options than just repeating the past. It is easy to over-complicate letting go, but it is simply a matter of cultivating your ability to see yourself clearly. If you cannot see yourself, then there is no other option but to continue reacting the way you have before. But being able to perceive that subtle space and pull yourself out of incessant reactions makes a huge difference. Being able to notice the initial reaction and then take your time to intentionally assess what is happening within helps you respond peacefully by observing your momentary emotions as opposed to getting swallowed up by them.

Resistance to Change

The most common response to change is resistance. We wish to maintain our youth and crave flawless health. We want the people we love to never leave us. We wish pleasant moments and easy times would always remain. The human mind will even go as far as to ignore that change is even a possibility so it can maintain the illusion of good things lasting forever. Our craving for pleasant things is sometimes so strong that we don't even want to acknowledge that tough moments are happening.

Resisting the flow of change will cause you an immeasurable amount of struggle. It is like trying to move upstream against the clear flow of a river. You can spend countless hours pushing against change with no real success—change will always win. If you were simply to let go and allow yourself to move with the flow of nature, you would still encounter occasional challenges, but you would not be adding as much mental pressure as before. If you want to build harmony in yourself, you need to allow yourself to live in harmony with this fundamental law. Embracing change is the path to alleviating and eventually eradicating suffering. Change is the truth that binds together the arc of the universe.

If you spend too much time fearing change, you will forget to celebrate it. Everything within the universe of mind and matter exists because of the movement of change. Every conceivable level—from the atomic, to the molecular, to the mental and the conventional level where human beings interact with each other on a daily basis—is constantly in motion. This pervasive, ephemeral quality is ubiquitous, impacting reality, whether we are aware of it or not. Without the undercurrent of change, life itself would not be possible.

Our relationship to change defines the level of peace in our mind. The wisest and happiest people I have met are continuously immersed in the truth of change. Since the weight of forever is no longer something they are chasing, they move easily through life's ups and downs, and treat each moment more genuinely than the average person.

A meditation teacher whom I look up to has been meditating for more than fifty years in the same Vipassana tradition I am a part of. He is one of the only people I have met who has no evident reaction when he ponders his own impermanence. His wisdom arises from his detachment from his sense of self and his focus on using his life as a vehicle for service. His ability to live beyond the ego actually makes him even more connected to life and the moments he dwells in. As we walked together one day, we spoke about the future, a future that would occur long after he was gone. In his words, there was no sadness, or words of caution, or attachments to how things should be done when that time came. He did not seek any type of glory, nor did he crave to be remembered. What stood out most was the unspoken happiness that shone from his long life of service and how the idea of his own death did not cause him any fear.

Since human beings have the vast majority of their awareness focused on the conventional level, it becomes easy to forget that changes big and small are always happening and are bound to continue occurring. The rapid speed of change at the atomic level is so hard for the mind to grasp that it becomes easy to ignore. The slower changes of planets and stars feel so far removed that they are also easily disregarded. Even in our personal lives, impermanence is an afterthought until something significant happens that makes this truth unavoidable. Difficult emotions feel like they are permanent when we are experiencing them, and we react to them as if they would last forever, forgetting that they will subside and others will take their place.

All the things we love come into being because the ups and downs of change have given them their shape. The people we cherish, the moments that bring us joy, the love we've felt, the victories that help us heal and live better—all these things are facilitated by change. If all things were static, there would be nothing new. Our very lives are the product of change.

Everything is impermanent, no matter how sweet or difficult. When the awareness of change matures, it washes away attachment and makes room for a loving presence that peacefully accepts that all things arise and ultimately pass away. While it is true that change is easy to recognize when it takes things away (endings are louder than beginnings), if we are to strike a healthy mental balance, we need to honor the fact that love, joy, and compassion—the sweetest parts of life—actually become stronger and clearer the more we embrace the reality of change. Instead of passively hating change, we are better off trying to understand it. Change may take things away, but it is also the great giver that fills us with happiness and wisdom.

Many mental struggles have their origin in the resistance to change. When the mind becomes attuned to change, dissatisfaction and mental struggle will naturally decrease. *One of our greatest mental enemies is the fight against change. So much of our inner tension stems from our attachment to keeping the pleasant parts of life the same, which eventually crashes upon the shores of change.*

Freezing time or erasing moments is simply not possible. To be able to let go properly and move with greater ease through the rolling hills of change, we should cultivate an appreciation of the continuous stream of beginnings and endings. Similar to how some people have moments when they intentionally feel gratitude, taking moments to remember that change is happening within us, around us, and that it will continue causing the ups and downs of life can have a positive impact on our mindset. Since change is something we can't escape, there is no other option but to fully embrace it.

Someone asked me recently, "If you can sum up in one word what you are learning in this life, what would it be?" It was something I had been thinking about a lot, so the answer came quickly: impermanence.

Change has easily been my greatest teacher, and my rejection of change has been my greatest cause of sorrow.

Before the healing, when I was constantly fleeing into the false sanctuary of pleasure, I remember that as soon as a pleasurable moment would pass or the party was over, my mind would not feel settled or satisfied. To quiet the withdrawal, I would go back to my room and numb myself with marijuana until I'd finally pass out. I didn't understand back then that the obstacle I kept crashing against was this intense determination to avoid mental discomfort, which was based on my rejection of change as a natural part of life. Sitting with the truth of change could have saved me much misery in those days, but ultimately that suffering made me seek the path that would help me live a better life. I didn't understand that when you fail to embrace change, a great moment actually loses its vibrancy because too quickly the mind starts to feel anxiety about it ending. Similarly, hard moments feel like endless punishment because change has not brought the mind into balance with the understanding that they, too, will eventually end.

Everything in the history of mind and matter has a beginning and an end. Our fear that endings will ruin the beautiful moments of life is actually counterintuitive. When we live with the truth of change, everything that is good becomes brighter and everything that is hard becomes more tolerable.

The Real You

There is a common misconception that the real you is only seen through your unfiltered thoughts and words, the you who emerges without any thoughtful processing. You hold up your immediate reaction on a pedestal. As a result, you believe that it defines your identity and reveals the core of who you are. In reality, this is completely untrue. The real you is not your initial reaction. The real you is your response that comes after your reaction. *The real you is the one who can weave out of the grasp of the past and produce an authentic response that is based in the present.*

Your initial reaction is your past revealing itself. Whether or not you are aware of it, how you felt before has been largely bottled up inside you. Your perception will measure everything you encounter in life today by its similarities to what you have felt in the past. If you see or feel something associated with a negative reaction, you will react in the same way in the present, even if your assessment of what is happening is exaggerated and incorrect. For the vast majority of us, our perception is completely colored by our past and our reactions seek to repeat themselves endlessly.

The mind moves so rapidly that it feels as if we are being authentic, when in reality we are letting our past experiences dictate how we feel in the present. Sometimes when we are triggered, we feel justified in expressing our anger by yelling or by loudly acting out our frustration, but this is not a sign of authenticity. This just reveals that we are caught in a cycle where our minds are overloaded with tension that keeps trying to feed its own fire. This is why slowing down and pausing will help us regain our footing in the present. Take a moment to process what is happening and align your actions with how you want to show up in the world. This is a much greater signifier of who you actually are than the random things your mind blurts out. Let go of the idea that who you are is whatever you impulsively do and recenter yourself on the fact that authenticity is a quality that requires strengthening and cultivation. Also accept that your authentic self can change and mature over time—you are not stuck in old ideas, patterns, and identities.

Being intentional is the same as being authentic. Staying in alignment with your values and with the version of yourself you are working on cultivating is the fundamental aspect of authenticity that opens the door to the real you. *Without intention, you would be aimless. Through intention, you reveal who you really are.*

To simply let your past self dominate your present-day thoughts, words, and actions is to miss out on fully living your life. Doing this means you are stuck in a loop where you are repeatedly replaying the past and strengthening patterns that don't necessarily enhance your happiness. Reinforcing the past keeps you stagnant, which may be easy in the moment because the past is familiar, but ultimately does not serve you well. The river of life wants to move you toward embracing change.

Attachments

The mind combats the natural flow of change by allowing most of its motivation to come from craving. Cravings quickly become attachments that try to mold reality into something it is not. Cravings are a rejection of reality as it is, and bring our focus into imagining what is missing or how we wish things would be. When our desire for things to be a certain way combines with tension, craving emerges. When we lock on to a particular idea and make our "happiness" dependent on it coming true, we are no longer living in the present moment—instead, we are striving to control reality. A continuous craving for things to be a certain way is known as "attachment."

A quick note: In this section and throughout the book, the word *attachment* is not meant in the common Western sense nor in the way it is described in the "attachment theory" of modern psychology. The understanding of attachment here is derived from the original Eastern sense that comes to us from the Buddha's teaching.

The attachments that the mind struggles with are born out of craving, and, as the Buddha realized 2,600 years ago, craving is the cause of our suffering. Craving is what keeps the mind full of tension and what keeps us far away from being fully present.

Hurt and attachment are bound together. When someone says something contrary to what we would like them to say—or, even worse, when what we are attached to no longer exists because the flow of time has eroded it—the pain we feel is tremendous. The more deeply we identify with something, the more our ego grabs hold of it. The lighter the attachment, the less hurt there will be. The deeper the attachment, the more mental pain there will be when it is challenged or taken away. The human mind doesn't just take in information, it evaluates that information and forms a relationship with it that is wrapped in tension. The mind is constantly creating images of the things it encounters and tying those images to a particular narrative. Through the accumulation of these narratives, we end up pushing reality further and further away. This is especially true when it comes to the people we love, as that love is often tangled up with attachments. We crave for our loved ones to live their lives in certain ways and make decisions that align with how we would decide things for ourselves. The love we have for dear ones is often tarnished by an inner push to control them, even when we know that real love is supporting their freedom.

I was the first person in my family to graduate from college. Traversing the unfamiliar terrain of the SAT, college applications, financial aid, and student loans without adult support felt overwhelming, but I managed to get through it. When the time came for my little sister to go through the same hurdles, I wanted to be a resource for her. I did not realize that I was far too attached to helping her. My eagerness would reveal itself in our conversations. I did a poor job listening to her and did not hold space for her well. She is an incredibly intelligent and independent person, but my craving to help her squandered a moment that could have brought us closer if I had just stuck to offering advice at the times when she was actually asking for it. She realized it would be best for her to figure out her own way through the process without my help and got accepted into a fantastic school. Fumbling that moment taught me to be less pedantic with her and to see her as an equal—to fully recognize her as an adult. Now our relationship has more harmony in it, because I focus on asking questions as opposed to teaching.

We get attached easily because we often exist in a state of constant reaction, where our mind is loudly or quietly making sharp assessments regarding whatever it encounters: I like this, I don't like that, I want more of this, keep this as far away from me as possible, and so on. Most of these snap judgments happen without us even noticing. We have obvious attachments to the things we crave, but we often miss the fact that we are also deeply attached to the things we hate or feel aversion toward.

Attachment itself is so alluring because it makes us feel that we can have security, that if we keep the things we crave close to us and defend our chosen narratives vehemently, we will be safe. Attachment itself is built on illusion, because most of the mental images we create and then rely on are based on narratives that are not fully truthful. Attachment has a seductive quality: Our mind is already inclined toward it, so why not continue moving in its direction? Even though it fills our minds with tension, we keep digging deeper into attachment to see if next time things will be different. If we just get this nicer material object or reach this next career milestone, or if others would just see us the way we want to be seen—with love and admiration—we think we will finally be happy. But the only certainties waiting for us are dissatisfaction and more craving. Attachment is a huge pattern, arguably one of the biggest. And each time we create another mental image that we wrap our identity around, we make the pattern thicker and more liable to occur over and over again. Seeing attachment as a form of security is one of the biggest mirages that human beings have fallen for. The reality is that there is no security in attachment—through it we will find nothing but pain, confusion, and misdirection. Real security can only be found in a deep embrace of impermanence.

Every attachment is a form of rebellion against impermanence. Wanting things or other people to exist in a very specific way is difficult to achieve when all we can truly control is our own actions. Clearly, we are all connected and influence each other in large and small ways, but even the richest person cannot control everything and everyone around them. Attachment often manifests in the mind first and then seeps into the external world as an attempt to control. Because everything is always changing, there is little chance for us to fulfill every craving that we have. If we are always being driven by our cravings, we are spending too much time in our imagination and far too little time in the present moment. Presence is possible when we are actively observing what is real within and around us. A deep presence requires not only self-awareness but also a degree of selflessness so that you can take in what is happening without projecting onto it.

In addition to understanding how craving is the cause of our suffering, the Buddha shined a light on our attachment to perfection and our deep craving for a life without troubles. The ups and downs of life are mainly out of our control, and waves will crash upon our life whether we want them to or not. No one knows what their future holds, but we know it will not all be blissful, or even all pleasant. There is an element of dissatisfaction that comes with being alive. Dissatisfaction is so deeply ingrained in the fabric of reality that it is virtually unavoidable, unless we eradicate the roots of ignorance, craving, and aversion that keep the mind wrapped in tension. This is possible, but it is an extraordinarily high goal, a state of supreme human evolution. But just because the suffering and dissatisfaction of life are realities, that does not mean that we can't cultivate our happiness amid the vicissitudes of life. We don't have to eradicate all suffering to make our lives happier and more peaceful. We can take this path step by step and benefit from our healing along the way.

This truth of suffering guides you inward and makes you wonder where the suffering begins; with proper insight it will point you to your own mental reactions. The truth of suffering may seem overwhelming and unavoidable, but it reflects your own power—it highlights the potential for real freedom and happiness. If suffering is real, so is happiness. If suffering is born out of ignorance, happiness can be born out of wisdom. If suffering is augmented by a lack of aware-ness, an increase in self-awareness can help you achieve a state of less mental tension.

Attachments thwart our path to happiness and fill our life with mental pain. Both our attachments and the truth of suffering point to the fact that letting go is our only path forward. There are certainly things we can control, but those are highly limited and much fewer than the ego would like to believe. If we want more harmony in our lives, if we want to have greater access to happiness, if we want to live in alignment with nature, we need to throw away the idea that attachment will bring us security and happiness. The only real way forward is the path of letting go. Even with the truth of suffering, once we let go of our craving for things to always be exciting, peaceful, and good, we give ourselves a greater amount of flexibility that will keep us from feeling so much mental pain when life gets tough.

A promising path to security, even though it may seem paradoxical, is letting go. When you are attached to nothing, there is no pathway to hurt. When you are attached to nothing, happiness appears in abundance. There is nothing passive or cold about letting go—it actually helps you live a much more active life, except that now you are living in alignment with the truth of impermanence. Yes, there are things and people you love, but they are always changing. They will be with you for some time, and eventually they, too, will be gone, just like everything else. If we embrace the truth of change, letting go becomes more clear-cut. We can enjoy things when they are around and we can help and be of service whenever possible, but we won't expect anything to last forever, especially in the same way that things currently exist, because that is simply not possible.

We can also have goals and plans for the future, but not expect to achieve all of them in a specific amount of time. When we stop fighting the truth of change, letting go of our attachments feels more natural, and, in the act of letting go, the love you have for whatever you hold dear will become purer because the element of control won't be as predominant. Serenity is possible when we are no longer carrying the ever-growing baggage of mental images, fueled by craving or aversion, everywhere we go. Without realizing it, we are weighing ourselves down by existing in a state of judgment—judgment of the present moment. These mental cravings become like rocks in the mind. If we recognize what we are holding on to, we have the opportunity to let it go.

The Control of Ego

Our ego is very helpful in survival settings, as we want to protect ourselves and those close to us. But once we pass that stage, the ego can be a great hindrance. The ego gives us a rigid sense of self and wants others to perceive us a certain way. The ego struggles to appreciate differences in opinions and views. One common cause of inner conflict is when someone close to us is making choices that we would not make ourselves. Our initial impulse is to want them to think and act like us. There is a sense of comfort the ego feels from uniformity: When our family, friends, and peers are all aligned with a particular view of what is right and what is wrong, we feel the pleasantness of safety and the reassurance that our view is correct. Our ego will make it seem like we are acting in their best interest by trying to convince them to behave or make decisions in a way we find agreeable, when, in reality, it is just the inflexibility of our attachment that is trying to get them to conform to what seems proper to us.

You crave for those close to you to be just like you, to see the world just like you, to think just like you. Your craving reinforces the ego's impulse to control and limits the flow of unconditional love that makes connections deep and fruitful. Love exudes the security and confidence to embrace differences. Love also helps you admit when you are wrong. It understands that our loved ones are complex and that control will never bring them closer to us.

People can come to an endless number of views and conclusions, which means the attachment to having others think just like us, or see us just as we want to be viewed, will never be fulfilled. There will always be differences in views and opinions, which are partially fed by different perspectives and the constant creation of nuances that expand our views. Decentering ourselves from our own perspective is a useful skill to develop because it allows us to more easily appreciate how someone else views things. The only option that supports our inner peace is to find a balance where we live our truth without trying to mold the people around us. We can certainly offer people our perspective, and it may even influence their decisions, but any advice is best delivered without the intention to control. Remember: You can ask someone to show up for you in a certain way, but you cannot force them to do anything. It has to be a voluntary agreement that arises out of their own volition.

Letting Go Takes Time

To be able to chip away at these old reactions that keep coming up and chart a new course in our behavior is a long road to travel. Often, the conditioning that we accumulate becomes dense and packs into the mind like hardened sediment from times long ago. Unconsciously, we carry these thick layers of concrete as patterns that keep affecting us in the present. It is completely possible to heal and let go, but it serves us best to be realistic about how much we carry inside us and how long it will take to fully rewire the mind. To be able to take on a fresh perspective and reframe old problems does not happen quickly. Healing is not possible without patience. And we must accept that letting go is a gradual process.

LETTING GO

if the pain was deep
you will have to let it go
many times

Letting go is not a one-time event; it is a habit that requires consistent repetition to become strong. Sometimes the reaction to the pain is so deep that we have to observe and release the tension repeatedly to fully cleanse the wound. Patterns for specific types of behaviors can be so firmly rooted that during our healing process we may feel that the same issues keep coming up for us to work on. We may even feel like we aren't making progress because of these persistent patterns, but in reality we are just getting the opportunity to release deeper layers of the same material.

The purpose of letting go is not to erase emotions, but to acknowledge their presence and transform your relationship to them. Before I began healing, my fear was that the sadness would always remain, but once I started embracing the truth of impermanence it became clear that, yes, the sadness had emerged and may stay around for some time, but it simply would not last forever. Understanding that it was only passing through made it more tolerable and less of a factor as I navigated my daily life. Being able to let go while a tough emotion is passing through helps us be okay with not being okay.

Letting go reaches deeper levels when your observation of what is happening inside you is done with total acceptance and when you remember that every part of life is impermanent. Especially in the mind, adding more tension to the tension that is already there will not make things better. When tension is met with unconditional acceptance, it has the space it needs to naturally unfold and release. Unloading and facing the mental weight of past hurt is never easy, but it is possible, especially when you feel ready for a great transformation.

Setting the Record Straight

A common fear is that letting go might make you passive. We are often so driven by our pain and fear that it is hard to conceive of any other way of existing. The reality is that letting go will not make you dull, and it certainly will not turn you into a pushover. What it does do is reconfigure your mind so that you are no longer carrying the heavy weight of the past into the present. If you are seeking to reclaim your power, one of the essential steps is realizing how much of your power you have given up to the hurt of the past and your fears of the future. Other key realizations include:

The heavy mental weight that you carry consumes a lot of your energy. Resisting, suppressing, or fighting your emotions on a regular basis quietly eats up your reserves. Living in a constant inner battle and treating yourself like an enemy pushes you far away from living at your most optimal level. Any mental tension will automatically consume energy, and when the added tension is removed, you'll feel a new vibrancy for life.

Letting go actually sharpens the mind by cleansing your perception. Letting go helps you see the moment you are in without the lens of the past dominating the way you perceive reality. A lighter mind and clearer eyes make space for wiser decision making. Your ability to act intelligently and authentically improves greatly the more you let go.

Letting go does not mean you give up on your goals. When you are able to relinquish the past and stop fearing the future, you gain a greater sense of awareness in the present moment, which will help you focus and think more effectively. Your best strategy to attain your goals will be more accessible when the weight of the past is no longer limiting your creativity. Letting go of craving quick results helps you get comfortable with the process of accomplishing new and difficult things. If you want to attain something great, you need to be ready for the long journey and able to adjust your strategy along the way.

Letting go does not erase the tough things that have happened. The key is to release the heavy attachments you have to these thoughts. The memories will still appear from time to time, even after deep healing has happened, but you know your effort has made a difference when you no longer react to these old memories with the same intensity as before. As a sign of victory, you can let tough thoughts and emotions pass without allowing them to dominate your mind or control your actions.

Letting go does not make you coldhearted. Letting go actually decreases self-centeredness and allows love to come forward much more unconditionally and with greater strength. It is hard to love yourself and others well when your mind is consumed with tension and craving control. Love shines brightest when it is shared in the present moment. When you put yourself through the process of letting go, you gain greater access to the here and now.

Ultimately, letting go is a mental state of clarity, where you no longer cause yourself extra suffering. Understanding that you can benefit from letting go is critical, but the next step is finding your practice so that you can start your own deep healing work. Wanting to let something go and having the tools to support you in this process are two very different things.

Reflection

In what ways do you make things harder for yourself?

What do you need to let go of? Does holding on make you feel safe, even though it hurts? Do you fear what life will be like after you let go? What more do you need to accept to fully let go?

What is your relationship with change? When you resist it, do you see how your mind bursts into tension?

Are you giving yourself the time you need to let go? Since letting go also takes intentional effort, are you making space to actively let go?

Does your ego want control?

How has your past influenced the way you react?

Are you giving yourself the time you need to respond intentionally to life, instead of letting your past speak through your reactions?

Chapter 4

Finding Your Practice

I went into Vipassana meditation because it had undoubtedly provided healing for my friend Sam, but I was especially impressed when I understood that it was a path of liberation.

My experience as one of the leaders of the Boston Youth Organizing Project (BYOP) in my late teens introduced me to how powerful a group of people can be. That was where I first grasped the idea of collective liberation in the context of undoing systems of oppression. But the inner liberation ideas of Vipassana focus on undoing the craving that causes suffering within the individual. Gaining this new understanding of personal liberation caused a cascade of connections for me. This is what I was missing. I knew how powerful it was to work with a group around a common cause, but I personally never felt any relief from the tension that was often flowing intensely in my mind.

At BYOP we addressed many citywide issues, from

changing the way guidance counselors interacted with high school students to getting the city to give young people free bus passes to securing more funding in the city budget for summer jobs for high schoolers. We were no strangers to gathering people, empowering them, and making tangible change in our city, but all these victories never penetrated the depth of my mind. They never helped me deal with my internal sadness and anxiety. No external success could heal my mind. Helping others certainly felt right, but I had yet to find a method to relieve my mind of all this pressure. As difficult as it was, after that initial ten-day retreat, my mind felt healthier and lighter than it had in a long time, and I knew I had found a different understanding of liberation. But it also complemented my original vision of the power of collective external liberation. Perhaps if more people take their healing seriously and find liberation within themselves, then we can also heal and bring more peace to the world.

For me, this practice continues meeting my healing goals, helps me take steps forward on the path of liberation, and encourages me to grow without pushing me too far into feeling overwhelmed.

The path that works for you may not be what another person needs. What works well for one may be the wrong fit for someone else's mind—or even just wrong at that particular moment. Healing requires you to find what works for you. Since we all have such unique conditioning, healing ourselves will require unique and individualized approaches.

Even when two people use the same practice, how quickly they move on that path and the difficulties and successes they encounter will be unique to the unfolding and healing of the emotional history they carry.

Everyone can have a more peaceful mind if they learn to let go, but the process of letting go will be different for each of us. Everyone reacts and each reaction leaves an imprint on the mind, but there are many different ways to do the work of unbinding and releasing these old patterns.

Fortunately, today there are an abundance of healing techniques that are more accessible than ever before. Healing, personal growth, and introspection have become so widespread that it feels like we are living through the beginning of a new renaissance for humanity. Has there ever been another period in recorded human history where so many people have been actively cultivating their self-awareness and inner peace? Has there ever been a time when so many have been reckoning with the past they carry and finding ways to undo personal and historical trauma? More people than ever before have time to focus on introspective pursuits.

One of the positive results of living in a globalized world is that the best practices from different cultures are now more widely accessible. Many techniques have been incubated and refined in their places of origin and are now spreading around the world. We also live in a period when the importance of mental health has transcended specific localities and become global. Discussions about mental health may have started off as a way to raise awareness, but they are now moving people to examine themselves deeply and engage with their own healing.

Not only are we more open to embracing our imperfections, but we are coming to terms with our traumas and old hurts in a big way. More of us can feel the way our past weighs down our present, and we are looking for ways to alleviate the tension in our minds because we know that doing so will improve every facet of our lives. The stigma surrounding mental health is decreasing. We don't need to hide the difficulties we face in our minds the way our parents used to. Society is now more welcoming to these deeper conversations which deal with what our minds need to move from simply surviving to thriving.

Whether it is in terms of healing yourself or seeking to develop your character in specific directions, having a mindset that embraces growth is no longer rare.

It is important to note that we have a ways to go in terms of creating more systemic accessibility so that healing is not just for those who have the time and money to pursue it, but for all people who are suffering, no matter what their economic background. We also have a ways to go with regard to respecting the traditions and peoples who have created and maintained these practices that are now spreading around the world.

Once you do find your practice, I trust you'll experience an immense amount of relief and even excitement. It can be quite thrilling to finally have a method that brings real results. There is nothing wrong with letting our enthusiasm lead and letting our friends and family know that we have found a practice that actually works. It is commendable to share good things with others, but we need to make sure that we do not develop a superiority complex. The ego can quickly grab a good thing and use it to create an imaginary hierarchy, where you view your practice as much better than all others and believe that your way is the only way for all people to heal. The reality is that it is not—your practice may work well for you, but it may be the wrong fit for someone else, and you may even outgrow it at some point.

Tips for Finding Your Practice

If you were to search HOW TO HEAL ANXIETY on Google, you would likely get over a hundred million results. The upside is that something is out there for you; the downside is that having so many choices can feel overwhelming. Some of the most popular healing techniques include one-on-one talk therapy, group therapy, psychiatry, yoga, mindfulness, light forms of meditation, and more serious forms of meditation. Within each of these practices, you'll find a wide spectrum of styles. On top of that, there are many more healing methods that people are deriving real results from, ones that are being newly developed and combinations of different techniques.

Before you begin your search, you need to ask yourself some questions: What are my healing goals? What patterns do I need to unbind and release? What type of practice am I interested in trying? Having an aim will help you narrow down the field and give your mind a clear trajectory of how it is going to evolve. As you try different methods, you need to check in with yourself and ask, "Can this practice help me move in the direction of my goals?"

The practice that is right for you will be something that you find challenging but not overwhelming. You have to locate your own sweet spot, where the practice is hard enough that it is helping you grow, but not so difficult that too many heavy patterns and old emotions are coming up all at once. These may cause you to feel overwhelmed and stop the process. The key is to settle on a practice that meets your conditioning where it is. You will also know that a method is for you because you will feel that you aren't wasting your time. The biggest sign is that your intuition will click and you will feel that this is something that you need to give your time to.

When you start exploring different practices, do not be discouraged if the first thing you try is not a perfect fit. For most people, it takes a bit of time and being openhearted to find what works. One thing you try may lead you to another, and, eventually, you will land on something where your intuition declares clearly, "This is it!" The other thing to consider is that once you do start your healing work, you may find that at some point you are ready to go deeper and naturally seek out a new method that can help you excavate subtler forms of old hurt.

Throughout your healing journey, your intuition will be the primary compass for you to follow. Many people may try to give you advice and you may see different things online, but if your intuition is not fully aligned with what you are doing, that is a clear sign it is not for you. People read their intuition differently, but, for me, it is a calm persistence that reveals itself as a knowing, as opposed to a craving. It feels more like a wholeness in the body that firmly points toward a particular decision, which is different from the mental chatter that our cravings will make in the mind. Intuition just knows, and the message is delivered without tension. Often, the message will calmly persist until I am ready to listen to its advice.

An important lesson for me has been seeing the people in my life walk different paths to improve their lives. I have family members and friends who have benefited greatly from therapy, some who have sought psychiatry and found it to be incredibly helpful, and many who practice meditation techniques other than the style of Vipassana that I practice, and they have made great progress in their evolution. Individuals will have different growth goals and seek to heal issues that are unique to their conditioning. There is nothing wrong with people moving at their own speed and taking on the internal challenges that they feel ready to handle.

How we take steps forward—and how many steps we

choose to take—depends on our personal conditioning. What matters is that help is out there. Taking steps forward in our personal evolution is now more possible than ever.

Trained help is always worth getting. There is no need to try to reinvent the wheel or to do it all yourself. Asking for help is a huge part of healing and demonstrates a lot of internal fortitude. If you want to learn how to meditate, learn from a trained guide who has a lot of experience. If you want to process your emotions intellectually and verbally, see a therapist. Leaning on experienced people will only make your healing journey more productive and efficient.

Be wary of techniques that promise fast results or miraculous effects and say they will do all the inner work for you. Our society is addicted to fast results and cure-alls, and this type of mentality can easily seep into our idea of healing. Real healing is definitely doable and life-changing, but it will take time—great transformations are normally things you will have to work for. And there is nothing wrong with that.

Another thing to watch out for is your own doubt. Doubt is one of the ways that your old patterns will try to defend themselves. The conditioning of the mind wants to just repeat the past over and over again, and it will try to reject new things. When you seek out a new technique, make sure to give it a fair trial and try it for a few weeks so you can really assess if it is making your mind feel lighter or more aware. You won't be able to properly assess if a practice is for you if you quit as soon as it gets hard. Give yourself the time you need to see whether or not it is right for you.

Others can help show you how to use a technique or talk you through building self-awareness, but none of that will compare to you reclaiming your power and activating the tools you were given by using your own effort. At the end of the day, you are the only person who can take steps forward on your healing path—no one else can do the work for you. People who are serious about deep healing are not afraid of the long journey.

Once you start the process of letting go and find a practice that makes the navigation of your internal landscape smoother, profound changes will begin. Knowing yourself ignites a process of transformation that helps you reclaim your power from your old human habits and return that power to your true human nature.

Reflections

What practices have you tried so far?

What healing techniques have you heard of that you've always wanted to try and intuitively feel might be right for you?

Are there any that feel right and that you should commit time and energy to?

What kind of results do you want to see from a healing practice?

Are you doubting your strength to do this serious inner work? Do you realize how powerful you truly are to have gotten this far?

Are you setting aside time for daily intentional healing?

Chapter 5

Human Habit versus Human Nature

The Western world has long maintained a bleak view of human nature, judging human beings as fundamentally self-interested and dominated by greed and assuming that at our core we think of ourselves first and others second. This assumption is so widely held that it greatly impacts the way our nations and companies interact at the macro level, as well as our interactions at the local level. The idea of greed as the innate motivator of the individual is so strong that "Greed is good"—the famous quote from the 1987 movie *Wall Street*—remains a cultural meme that gives voice to the way many people feel about the value of self-interested thinking and behavior.

On the surface, it may appear true that people are inherently selfish. Human history reveals numerous instances of collective behaviors that were initiated by greed and resulted in great harm. Wars for the expansion of power, the colonization of people to turn their land into sources of wealth, enslavement and dehumanization as a way to generate profit, the massive gap between rich and poor—there is no shortage of examples of how greed motivated actions that ended up creating devastation. The real world is still largely controlled by this old idea of human nature, as evidenced by the endless drive for profit that is pushing our global climate into dangerous territory.

Even on the individual level, there is a lack of trust among people. The idea of the dangerous stranger remains pervasive, because we fear that their greed or malice may cause us harm. Because we do not know each other, we find it much easier to distrust one another and focus purely on our own self-interest and that of our inner circle.

There is no doubt that greed is real and that it is having a clear impact on the way we interact at the group and individual levels. But to think that this is our true and sole nature and that there is nothing that can be done about it reflects a superficial understanding of what it means to be human. It carries a defeatist tone that does not give credit to humanity's powerful ability to change.

This idea of greed as our basic human nature does come from a rational place. Craving and aversion are the great motivators of human thought, speech, and action—the Buddha pointed this out clearly in his teaching. But that is not all that we are. On the surface, it may look like this is our true nature, because it is currently rampant throughout the world. But the reality is that greed is a conditioned habit that is easily mistaken for our true nature. The selfishness of greed is deeply rooted in the mind, but it is a pattern like any other—it can be observed and released.

What was once widely understood as human nature—being greedy, fearful, and even hateful—is not our nature at all. These traits are human habits, conditioned behavior that was imprinted onto us by past generations and past experiences. The trauma we carry and the ways we have blindly reacted throughout our own lives are often picked up from when we were struggling through the more difficult periods of life, while we were set on survival mode. *Ultimately, human habit is survival mode.* Human habit is not permanent, and it is not who we are at our core. Our real human nature is what shines brightly underneath all the patterns, old pain, and confusion that stops us from being the best version of ourselves. Our real human nature is love, mental clarity, creativity, and a zest for life that is informed by the past but no longer weighed down or controlled by it.

We live in the early stages of a new era of global healing. Human history has not yet known healing on such a vast global scale. The moment we are in is radically unprecedented. Throughout all of history, there have been individuals and groups of people who have tried to change the world for the better, to expand rights and create a more humane design for our social structures. But this is the first time that healing is also widely accessible to the individual. Many people who are alive today continue the work of trying to change the world for the better, but now we also have methods available to us that can help us substantially transform ourselves as we simultaneously work on transforming the world. This will be the moment when change-makers will be able to unbind their human habit and have more access to their human nature.

If we scale up the healing of the individual and multiply it by millions, it will cause a cultural shift in our understanding of what defines human nature. This will not be driven by what we say, but by how we show up in our daily lives. The layers of human habit are certainly thick, and they are not easy to overcome, but with patience, intentional action, and good healing methods we can unbind them enough for true human nature to come forward and shine brightly.

Who do we become after we have peeled back the layers of greed and fear that have dominated our lives and stood in the way of our happiness? How do we feel and think after we have come to terms with our old pain and start the work of deep healing? Who are we after we are no longer dominated by selfishness? What does a mind feel like when it no longer carries so much burden?

One of my favorite stories from the Buddhist Suttas, told by S. N. Goenka during his ten-day meditation course, shines light on our innate nature. A man named Angulimala, who was a savage killer during the time of the Buddha, had killed 999 people and was on the lookout for his 1,000th victim. His mind was so warped by ignorance and harmful conditioning that he was not fully aware of the horror he was causing. All he could think about was the next person he would kill. But he could not fully grasp the devastation he was causing because he did not have access to the compassion that was buried under such heavy conditioning. When he encountered the Buddha, he intended to kill him but was not able to. Instead, the Buddha got Angulimala to listen to him, and Angulimala embraced meditation and the deconditioning process. He learned about himself and penetrated the deepest truths of nature. In the same lifetime he became a fully liberated saint—a person who no longer causes themselves suffering or reacts blindly. Saints have no motivation whatsoever to cause harm to themselves or others. He went deeply inward and the rough layers of human habit were burned away. All that was left was the clarity of a human being who was fully connected to the unconditioned nature that all people can access within.

This story highlights two critical aspects of what it means to be human. One is that even people who commit horrible acts are never fully lost or permanently dangerous. Everyone has the innate capacity to enter into a transformative process to free themselves of behavior that harms others and stop the patterns that do not serve their personal wellbeing. The second is that the roughest aspects of your character do not fully define who you are. The outer shell may be thick and prone to harmful or defensive behavior, but underneath there is a vast pool of loving clarity waiting for you to access it. If you do the work, the brightness of your true human nature will reveal itself.

Accessing your human nature is not easy. We all have such different conditioning that we can't compare our personal journey with another's. We can certainly be inspired by the progress others make, but we can't expect to move on the same time line or for the tools that work for someone else to work in the same way for us. What is helpful is that the path of letting go and healing is no longer a mystery. You just have to go out there and find what helps heal your old conditioning in a way that suits you well.

letting go can feel like a tremendous struggle
even when you know that it is absolutely necessary
for you to live a better life
breaking with the past is literally a break
an end
a refusal to return
old patterns keep repeating until you intentionally
move in a new direction

Human Habit as Survival

The default mode of the mind is survival, meaning it is mainly motivated by fear, craving, aversion, and self-centeredness—this is the initial layer of human habit. Many of these habits stem from encoded evolutionary direction to help keep us safe and survive long enough to pass along our genes. Being cautious and greedy can have its survival advantages. But living simply for survival in the modern world is incredibly limiting. When you train the mind to observe things as they really are, to take in reality without projecting your emotions onto it and without trying to control it, happiness will become more available to you—this is how you open yourself up to your loving human nature. Happiness requires intentional action, healing, letting go, and teaching the mind to settle into the present moment. Only the effort that comes from you can activate your happiness.

Take a moment to think about the last time you felt rough emotions, like anger, anxiety, stress, fear, worry, or sadness. Was there an external event or trigger that brought them up? Do you find yourself repeating this mental pattern when in similar situations? Do the same types of situations get a similar reaction out of you? We get stuck in these cycles over and over again, which only solidifies them even more in our subconscious. Often, this happens when we find ourselves in a situation over which we do not have control. We immediately revert back to human habit as a way to protect ourselves. Understanding your patterns, and being aware of what types of situations cue them, takes a lot of their power away. Our perception is so loaded with past information that we often match new experiences with old ones so that our minds can make sense of what is happening. Each time we do this, we create a pathway for us to react in a way we have in the past. Human habit is essentially the sum total of your patterns, while true human nature is a mind that is no longer governed by patterns. It still contains the information of the past to help you make good decisions, but that information is no longer in command. Instead, you are now inclined toward observing what is happening without immediately jumping into a defensive stance.

Left to its old patterns, the mind will continue its reactivity and keep you functioning on autopilot. What the mind knows best is unconscious repetition, especially when difficult situations arise. This keeps you in survival mode, which defaults into blind behavior.

Human habit is often a state of confusion, where the way we react is fast and blind. We don't understand why certain patterns are so dominant in us and why we spend more time with some emotions than others. You know you are still run by your human habit when your inner world continues to feel like a mystery to you, especially if it feels like a mystery that you don't feel ready to explore and solve. In the state of human habit, it is hard to know what we want to do with our lives, and it is easy to confuse what we have picked up from society, the media, or our parents as our true aspirations. As strange as it sounds now, there was a time before I started healing that I thought about being an investment banker. I thought that maybe it would be the instant fix for my family's poverty. But it would have cured only the surface-level issues. I know now that, if I had taken that route, my internal issues would have cascaded into an even bigger rock bottom. Many people find that once they start healing and accessing their human nature, they drop their old goals because they were never really theirs to begin with. Often an individual's real aspirations that are hidden under their old human habit are more creative, more in service to others, more focused on improving society. The other side of things is that you don't need to quit your job to take your healing seriously. My wife, Sara, is a good example of this; she kept her job as a scientist who designs experiments, even as she blossomed as a meditator. Each person needs to figure out what works best for them. You don't need to be fully liberated, like Angulimala, to experience a profound and life-changing transformation. Even healing yourself a small amount will radically alter your life and help you find your authentic aspirations that fully click with your intuition.

Human habit is prevalent in us when our mind focuses too much on the past or the future. Since human habit is strongly connected to survival, our record of the past will be the main filter that we use to assess the world. Rather than taking in what is happening in a fresh way and without judgment, we will make quick evaluations and not have the patience to fully grasp the novel and complex quality of each individual moment. Our thoughts of the future will be similarly molded by whatever happened in the past. And our anxieties and concerns will be on a mission to make sure that the things we hated from the past do not happen again, even if there is very little possibility of them recurring. To break the loop of getting caught in anxiety, driven by past emotional hurt, we must come in contact with our emotions as they arise in the present moment.

Your real human nature is found in the present moment, and many of the most powerful experiences available to a person can be found there: wisdom, love, joy, healing, happiness, and peace. While these can be superficially accessed through memories or by imagining the future, to experience the full power of them you have to feel them in real time. When your attention is in the present moment, the door to your human nature is open. The mind becomes more stable, less driven by false narratives, and better able to connect with peace easily. To be fully happy and wise requires mental training, and most of that training revolves around having the patience to repeatedly pull yourself out of senseless narratives, driven by tension, and back to reality.

If you continuously reject what you feel, the emotions you ignore will actually harden in your mind and make the turbulent feelings you are trying to avoid more prominent. Avoidance may seem like the right answer in the moment, especially when you are in survival mode, but as you repeat this reaction of avoidance it will only make this pattern stronger. *If your strategy is to avoid, it will make the distance between you and yourself wider and wider. At first, this strategy will feel like relief, but later it will feel like you are no longer at home within your mind and body.* This space between you and yourself does not remain empty. It fills up easily with more narratives that are driven by craving, fear, aversion, and misunderstanding— essentially more of the mental material that creates that rough top layer of human habit. When we continuously re- peat the strategy of avoidance, it becomes easier and more automatic to fall into, even if the emotions that arise are not at their highest intensity. Through avoidance, we end up be- coming alienated from ourselves.

The True Beauty of Human Nature

Allowing yourself to feel your emotions without running away is the gateway to entering into healing and the path to accessing your human nature. When you break down the layers of old conditioning, your inner revolution begins. You experience the revival of a mind that is no longer heavily weighed down by the past. Your eyes light up and your mind starts to feel fresh and energized. When old, heavy emotions arise for further processing and release, you deal with them with a new grace—you feel your emotions without giving them all your power.

Healing does not make all the pain go away, and often it is a slow process that takes patience and commitment. What makes this journey worth it is that even small amounts of healing can make a difference in our lives. When you start saying no to old patterns and choosing actions that better align with how you authentically feel, your human nature starts to shine through. In a dark room that is lined with concrete, if a small hole is made, the darkness will no longer be all-consuming. In a similar way, if we keep chipping away and breaking down the walls of old conditioning that confine us, more light will get in and we will be able to see the outside world with a wider and clearer perspective.

There is a wealth of energy and creativity that flows beneath the hardened layers of human habit. So much energy is burned away through worry, anxiety, and falling into the loops of false narratives, but a healed mind has a pristine and flexible quality that allows us to see things from more perspectives than just our own. Using present-moment awareness to activate your human nature gives you access to an abundance of mental clarity. Clarity and creativity are really one.

When the mind is unburdened, it can see things from many angles and dissect situations with greater ease. It can see beyond the superficial and discover what is missing without causing itself tension. A calm mind that has slowly become unconditioned and relieved of old patterns has an easier time connecting with beauty and finding solutions.

Ultimately, activating your human nature gives you access to your full power. You feel more, see more, and solve more. At first it may even feel superhuman because your mind feels like it has a higher degree of intelligence, but this is your natural, unburdened state.

Human Nature Is Open to All of Us

Historically, this transition from human habit to human nature is nothing new. Great figures from across time have used periods of introspection to connect with liberational truth. Through their growing self-awareness, they were able to activate their human nature. This allowed the innate clarity of love and the power of peaceful creativity to flow abundantly in their own lives and for the benefit of those whose paths they crossed. Jesus spent forty days in the desert in deep reflection and overcame doubt. The Buddha spent six years practicing different techniques until he was able to fully liberate himself from all conditioning. The methods were different but there is a similarity in the results. Through introspection and by deeply connecting to what was real inside each of them—what is also real inside each one of us—they became beings of boundless love, experienced the freedom of egolessness, and were able to access an exceptional degree of wisdom.

To be able to love unconditionally and fully eradicate suffering within the mind is a high achievement. It is possible, but it is a serious path that takes determination and effort. Even though we may be far from that level of pristine freedom, that should not discourage us. Those of us alive now can still see those achievements as a form of inspiration. The examples of Jesus, the Buddha, and others remind us that we have the same potential within us. Even if we tread slowly into doing introspective work, we can make progress that can radically transform our lives for the better.

There are plenty of examples of people who have struggled immensely with mental tension, picked up one introspective method or another, and come out the other end with an undeniable connection to their human nature. When we chip away at our old human habit and truly understand that it is composed of knotted-up patterns that are just as impermanent as anything else, we can develop the patience to calmly undo them by building new responses to life.

•

keep unbinding the past that weighs down the mind
let go of the tension that limits your ability
to wholeheartedly enter into the present
heal the fear that stops you from aligning
with your highest goals
—this is how you stay committed to your growth

The difference in your state of mind, from when you began your journey to how it is now, is significant. But mental qualities that support your thriving are never won easily; they have to be constructed patiently because they are to become the foundation for your new life. The lightness, clarity, and skill you have from observing yourself took time and intention to build, but now they are yours. Taking a step back from serious inner work so you can take a good look at how far you have come helps put things in perspective and gives you the boost you need to keep going. Better moments are here, and even better days are on their way.

As you do the deconditioning work that helps your mind become lighter, less traumatized, and less dominated by your old human habit, your human nature becomes more predominant. The innate qualities of a healed mind become easier to access, but even so they are like seedlings that have just burst into the sunlight. These qualities can breathe now, but they are not yet mature. As you cross this threshold, it is important not to expect a continuous flow of present-moment awareness or a constant positive energy for life: There will continue to be ups and downs.

The key to taking more steps forward as the best version of yourself is repetition. Practice love for yourself and others, and it will become stronger; pull yourself out of your perspective to take a look at how others see things, and you will empower your mental agility; intentionally feel happiness for the success of others, and jealousy will lose its power;

take time to feel gratitude and eventually your mindset will flow in that direction more easily.

The qualities that can support your happiness become available when you use your present-moment awareness to live from a space of human nature. Even so, you need to take time to strengthen those qualities so that you can continue elevating the parts of your mind that help you thrive. When you understand the malleability of your mind, you bring energy to your courage and start to take back your power from the past.

Reflections

In what ways has your conditioned human habit made life harder?

What does your mind feel like when you are connected to your human nature?

Are you able to persevere even when it is difficult to connect with your human nature and cultivate those good qualities that can help improve your life?

How has your ability to problem-solve changed since you started your healing journey? Are you seeing more creativity flow into your life?

Do you have faith that you can become the person you know you can be?

Who is an example in your life who does a good job living from a space of loving human nature?

Chapter 6

Emotional Maturity

Emotional maturity is an expansive term, but I define it here as "continuous growth": the lifelong journey that we are all on to improve the way we relate to our emotions, especially in how we reclaim our power from our past and cause ourselves less mental tension. Emotional maturity is not about perfection. Instead, it's about making progress in our healing practice, building up self-awareness and compassion, and not reacting as strongly as we have been to difficult situations. Enhancing your strength in any of these areas is a reason for celebration. Do not be hard on yourself for not having it all perfected—what matters is that you are moving forward in your journey.

Self-awareness. Emotional maturity begins when you turn your attention inward. Cultivate the ability to see yourself as you move through the vicissitudes of life without running away or suppressing what comes up in your mind. This will immediately enhance your understanding of yourself.

Signs that your self-awareness is growing:

Being able to feel your emotions as they come and go

Coming to terms with your past and noticing the way it shows up in your present

Watching your mind as it processes difficult situations

Taking note of behavior patterns that show up repeatedly in your life

Observing how your own thinking affects your emotions

Examining your inner narrative

By paying close attention to these mental movements, you'll open the door to the type of learning that can transform your life. Your ability to see yourself through the lens of radical honesty is the foundation of emotional maturity, and this vantage point will help you make decisions from a place of active clarity, instead of a place of passive unconsciousness.

Non-reaction. Building your self-awareness increases the agility of your mind. When you make time to be present, it becomes possible to slow your mind down when difficult situations arise. Instead of falling back into blind reactions that are rooted in your past, you can intentionally lean into pausing and give yourself a moment to take a look at what is actually happening. This ability to pause is not easy and it takes practice to develop, but the results are immense. Not reacting functions as a medium for greater emotional maturity. Now that you can see yourself and give yourself time, you can more easily behave in ways that align with your goals and honor your authenticity. Finding that balance—where you can be honest about what you are feeling and not allow this temporary emotion to take total control of your actions—can help you better handle the unexpected changes of life. Non-reaction is essentially a practice in patience. The patience you are building will permeate your mind and open up your perception. Instead of perceiving things through a lens of judgment, you will be better able to embrace the way the long journey of developing emotional maturity slowly reveals and helps you accept your imperfections.

Compassion. When you are making use of your new self-awareness and no longer reacting to every challenging situation the same way you used to, it becomes a lot easier to feel love and compassion for yourself and other people. Additionally, now that you can see yourself better, you will naturally be able to see others more clearly. As you better understand yourself, your inclination to punish yourself for mistakes will decrease. As you see others struggle with their patterns, learn more about themselves, and move through their own ups and downs, it will become easier to feel compassion for them because you, too, have gone through these steps and know how challenging the process can be. Emotional maturity gives you the strength to see things outside your own perspective. Being able to place yourself in another person's shoes and see their context is an active form of compassion.

Growth and healing. Your emotional maturity deepens when you can acknowledge that you have much to learn and heal. Making an active commitment to your personal evolution, whether that is specifically working on letting go of old trauma or focusing on developing new positive habits, will open you up to deeper levels of wisdom and peace. One of the hardest battles to overcome is simply having enough courage and inner security to adopt a lifestyle that supports your evolution and mental health. Once you make this lifelong pledge to grow, your task will be to apply effort so that you can remain on the path. Emotional maturity is a lifelong practice in humility and persistence, because you understand that your immediate thoughts are not always correct and that it is worth your time to patiently investigate the roots of your patterns. At its core, emotional maturity is a matter of improving your communication with yourself. This ongoing commitment to yourself will also enhance outward connection and communication with others.

Avoidance Is the Opposite of Emotional Maturity

When you can't handle your own pain or the turbulence of your emotions, it is easy to fall into a cycle where you use others as a means of escape. Spending time with others as a way to avoid yourself is a common pattern when the hurt feels too heavy to carry, or when you have not yet found a clear healing method that works for you. Sometimes avoiding yourself is an unconscious pattern, where you focus so much on what is outside of you that you do not have the self-awareness needed to see what is motivating your behavior.

This idea should not be taken to an extreme; being in community can be very healing and human beings are naturally interdependent. What you should be alert to is the constant avoidance of solitude. There is also nothing wrong with having a friend help you take your mind off something that is too heavy to process at the moment, but a clear sign of being disconnected from yourself is when too many of your relationships are driven by your need to dodge your tension.

In the past, my way of avoiding myself was by forging a deep attachment to pleasure. It is a common escape route when we don't know how to manage our own pain. If our past feels overwhelming or our pattern of avoidance is deeply rooted, it becomes easy to fall into unhealthy habits in pursuit of the sensation of pleasure. A deep attachment to pleasure can produce a heavily self-centered frame of mind. For some, their escape mechanism may be always surrounding themselves with people or work. For others it may be overeating, watching too much TV, drug abuse, or any other extreme that keeps them saturated in the sensation of pleasure and away from fully engaging with reality.

The act of running away from yourself has clear consequences in your relationships. If you do not know yourself well, it will be hard to deeply love and understand those around you. If you cannot meet yourself in total honesty, it will be difficult to hold space and go deep with others. If you do not have compassion for yourself, it will be hard to treat others well. Full honesty, while difficult at first, can stabilize the groundwork of relationships by building trust and understanding.

Relationships that are solely based on excitement, pleasure, and seeking the next thrill tend to be pretty surface-level and do not stand the test of time. Full-spectrum connections have space for enjoyment, deep discussions, and truth sharing—they have a foundation of patience, where each person is willing to truly listen. There is nothing wrong with having fun, but living solely for fun will leave you feeling empty.

A common thread for many, once they start building self-awareness, is that they see how surface-level and superficial a lot of their relationships were. A process of intuitive analysis starts when you recognize which relationships you should bring more energy to and which ones you need to let go of. As your inner light starts shining more brightly, your circle of connections sometimes becomes smaller, but you feel prepared to bring more intentional presence into each interaction.

When you start journeying through your own inner landscape, self-awareness is activated and the door to wisdom opens up. This unbinding of old layers propels your evolution. The fact that you are no longer a stranger to yourself helps you make your connections richer and more mutually fulfilling. And often you make new connections along the way, ones more aligned with your path and your values.

Signs of Emotional Maturity

A key aspect of emotional maturity is making healthy sacrifices that support your long-term well-being more than your short-term pleasure. For example, you give time to your healing, even when it is hard. You make space for rejuvenating connections, even when your craving wants to pull you back into old connections that you know are unhealthy for you. You embrace the repetition of good habits, even when it feels like they are building up slowly. You do the courageous work of keeping your heart open because you know that's the only way to forge deep and meaningful connections. You try to take in the present moment with a fresh perspective that isn't being constantly evaluated against what happened to you in the past.

More than anything, you give yourself what you need, instead of what you crave. Treating your energy like a precious resource has a deep effect on your life. Saying no becomes more common so you can focus your time and give it to your highest goals. You miss out on some events because you don't need as much external stimulation to make you feel fulfilled. And your fulfillment is now derived from your self-care and the wholeness that is uncovered from your healing work. You do remain open to healthy connections, but you are intentional about those you let into your inner circle. You give more time to your rest so that you can prosper while you are in the midst of your journey. Emotionally mature people are kind and gentle toward others, but they give the highest priority to what helps them thrive. Here are a few other ways you will know you are on the right track.

You don't need to jump into every argument or give your opinion on every matter. Sometimes you need to speak up in self-defense or to reaffirm boundaries, but saying less can make what you stand for much clearer and it will save your energy for moments when you know your words will have a great impact. Often, the urge to speak is ego-driven and may even bring greater friction to the situation. Being skillful and taking the time to understand where you are coming from before you speak is valuable. Is it from a place of impulse and reaction that seeks dominance? Or is it from a place of curiosity that seeks to build understanding between two people? Are you really listening to others or just planning what points you want to make next?

You have a strong sense of determination. One of the practices that has made the biggest difference in my own life is having the resolve to stick to a path of healing once I determined that I had to change. There are a lot of ways to grow, but whenever you want to take a new path seriously there will be a point where you have to put your foot down and say to yourself, "No one and no situation will stop me from moving in this new direction. Moving this way is what is best for me and I will no longer compromise my well-being." Having that strong determination has helped me become a daily meditator as well as pursue writing as a career.

As your self-awareness grows, the internal debate that occurs when you have an important decision in front of you becomes simpler and the decision you should make becomes more obvious. The struggle about which way to go and where to devote your time becomes less intense and time-consuming when you are no longer a mystery to yourself. Since you know your aspirations and have practice being your authentic self, whatever comes near you that does not align with your goals will not be able to stay around for long. Your self-awareness strengthens your intuition. As you make more progress, you will know what is for you and what is not for you.

You notice that similar emotions attract. Emotions usually attract similar emotions, and what you give to others in interpersonal situations is normally what you will get back. When you're feeling down and anger starts to suffuse your mind and actions, that makes it much easier for others to react to you with anger, since they feel justified in doing so. Similarly, if you are deep in your vulnerability and expressing it honestly, others will have an opening to respond with compassion and understanding. The emotion that you are expressing will often activate that same emotion in another person. When people are angry, they are often coming from a place of deep fear and hurt—something is triggering their need for survival and activating their human habit of anger as a form of protection. The higher work of someone who has deepened their healing and cultivated their emotional maturity is not getting pulled into unnecessary arguments when someone else is trying to spread their tension. With mental patience and agility, you can override your survival instinct of reacting to their tension with your own tension. When you use your self-awareness to override your survival instinct, you are saying no to human habit and yes to your human nature. From the space of human nature, it is easier to be gentle, to see other perspectives, to express love, to be more creative, and to have compassion and understanding, while still being able to defend yourself if necessary. Acting from a place of human nature does not make you passive; it makes you skillful in your approach to dealing with difficult situations.

You act with an increasing sense of responsibility. Accepting responsibility for your healing and happiness is incredibly difficult, but it is the only path available to us that can lead to inner peace, mental clarity, and sustainable happiness. If you believe that every moment of tension in your mind is always someone else's fault, then it will be difficult to feel substantial happiness or real peace. The ocean of life will push you here and there until you raise your sails and navigate through the waves that try to hold you back. There are undoubtedly hard moments in life, but the movements of your mind do not have to remain unconscious. How you perceive things does not always have to be dictated by what happened in the past. Instead, you can become more attuned to the present by bringing your mind out of your imagination and into what is actually happening inside you and in front of you. Building the foundation for a better life starts with what is happening inside your mind. People may push and test you, but cultivating a pillar of inner balance will help you remain sturdy when the world outside you is chaotic.

You learn to say no. When you make your goals a top priority, it will mean saying no to things that don't align with your vision. This is a sign that you have a clear view of where you are heading. Knowing what your real aspirations are will make your journey forward clear, so that you don't get pulled into distractions. Staying aligned is key because it is far too easy to use your energy in ways that do not support the best outcomes for the future you. Since every human being only has a finite amount of energy and time, it becomes incredibly important to have a serious conversation with yourself and ask: What do I want to do with my life? What do I want my mind to feel like a decade from now? What do I need to do now so that I can thrive later? Giving the greater share of your energy to your goals is not selfish. It means you know yourself so deeply that there is no confusion as to what truly matters to you and what you are currently building.

Part of self-improvement is saying no to good things to make more space for the type of work or opportunities that really get you fired up. Not settling for less is one of the most direct ways for you to embody the principle of self-love. Living up to your dreams or sticking to a greater mission is much more mentally difficult because it is easier to pick low-hanging fruit. Saying no will organize your boundaries in a way that points you to what will actually give you the deepest sense of fulfillment.

When you harness the power of being okay with walking away, you are reaffirming your true worth and opening doors you may not yet see. Something is not right for you if you know deep down that you will have regrets in a few weeks or months. Normally, your intuition will jump at an opportunity that is meant for you—it will not need a lot of convincing or pondering. You will feel the click and know that this is the next chapter of your story that is starting to unfold. Saying no to things that do not honor your worth may feel like a great risk, but you are better off moving with patience so that the right people and opportunities fully align.

You maintain humility. Humility is admitting to yourself that you can benefit from personal growth. It's a clear sign of inner strength, but it's not easy, since the ego struggles to see anything beyond its own perspective. A clear sign of emotional maturity is noticing when your ego is jumping to conclusions and then holding yourself back from making a quick judgment. An ego that has grown large is naturally full of tension and too fragile to recognize when it is wrong. Knowing that you have much more to learn helps keep your ego in check. Knowing that others always have something to teach you keeps you from condescension and harsh judgment.

There is a fine line between confidence and overconfidence. The ego always tries to stretch itself beyond what it understands, giving everything it encounters an evaluation, even when we have very little information on the person, subject, or situation to make a proper assessment. Instead, evaluate what you truly understand and have the internal fortitude to inquire about the rest. This is also important to remember when you are going through a slow moment or a tough time, as the ego often reverts to attacking itself when your mood is down. You will get a clearer picture of yourself when your mood has leveled out. Having the humility to remind yourself that hasty assessments are not helpful is a good practice. Judgment is heavy; keeping an open mind will help you flow more smoothly through life.

Disagreements

Real maturity is keeping your peace in the midst of a disagreement. A calm awareness will help you make sure that you are stating your point without letting your ego make things worse. This way, you are less likely to let a bad moment turn into a bad day and you will stop your tension from negatively affecting those around you. Your peace has the power to stop a disagreement from escalating into an argument. It takes two people to intensify a disagreement to the point where it becomes a real conflict; if you refuse to conduct yourself with tension it will help the conversation remain civil.

Thinking of your disagreement as a discussion is more productive than letting it snowball into an argument because a discussion is an exchange, as opposed to a battle. In a discussion, the ego does not need to guard itself and logical thinking can be more easily sustained. Keeping your peace will also help your mind remain open and flexible, which allows a resolution to arise more easily. Disagreements among people are a natural part of life that can open the door to a deeper understanding of each other. When we navigate opposing views with compassion, it becomes possible to deliver our perspective gently and to find a middle path. Remember, harmony does not appear out of nowhere; it often blossoms from the rocky ground of disagreements. Being able to hold space for different perspectives is a sign of true love.

You can tell when someone is sending you their misdirected anger. People often share their misery, even if you have nothing to do with it. Emotions tend to propagate themselves: Anger likes to create more anger and joy seeks to create more joy. When you notice that someone is just stuck in a loop of agitation and they are no longer open to reason, step away from them and move along. You can have compassion for them without getting caught up in their rough energy. Being able to dictate your own mental state without letting others decide it for you is a sign that you are reclaiming your power. Even if someone is inviting you to be angry, you do not need to accept their invitation.

The goal is to be able to skillfully maneuver around people who are in a turbulent mood without losing your cool. There will certainly be times when you can help them, but that won't always be the case. In any scenario, your task is to do what is right for your own mental health. Remember: Do not get stuck in a savior pattern. Help people when you can without becoming attached to being a helper; it is not your job to save everyone. Finding this balance will be unique to your life and your personal emotional capacity.

Intuition

One aspect of emotional maturity that is often undervalued is the ability to listen to our intuition. We all feel our own intuition differently. For me it appears as a quiet knowing that persists until I follow through on it, even if this means taking a considerable leap or a large risk. It is easy to let fear corral us into a small space that doesn't give us the room we need to flourish. But our intuition often moves in a way that allows us to break out into the world and fulfill our deepest aspirations. Intuition is not grounded in fear and it does not feel like the endless cravings that swirl in the mind. It feels like the body has a calm compass and it knows where to go next, even if that knowledge causes the mind to recoil with fear and aversion because you have to do something that is totally outside of your comfort zone.

When I was living in Boston and my healing journey was underway, there was a very clear moment when my intuition spoke to me with exacting directions. At this time I was slowly reclaiming my power and was no longer under the sway of heavy drugs. I had taken a few Vipassana courses and was generally happier and more connected to the love that was flowing within me. I was open to moving further along on my healing journey, and my intuition let me know it was time to leave Boston and move to New York City so I could continue growing.

I had actually tried to move there a year before, but it

had not worked out. My friends wanted me to come join them, and I had even gone as far as to move in with my friend Shin for a few weeks and start looking for a job. But as soon as I arrived, everything about my decision felt totally wrong. I loved New York and my friends, but something within me kept saying it was not right yet. However, this time things were different. I had never felt such clear support from within, and it was not just support. It felt like a clear instruction: "The next step is NYC." I talked to my partner, Sara, and she agreed that we should take on this new adventure and see what awaited us there. The way things aligned really made sense, as I was far enough into my healing journey that I did not feel like I would get shaken or thrown off my path by immersing myself in that intense environment. I had also made a new friend named Anwar at a meditation course. He also lived in NYC and it made me realize that I could not only keep my old friends but make new ones who were even more aligned with the healthy lifestyle that I was trying to build.

It took a lot of courage to leave Boston, as both my partner and I had jobs there, but we felt that our time there was up. Boston didn't have the same opportunity for career growth or community support we were looking for. We had to take the classic risk of leaving something good for the chance at something better. When we arrived in New York this time, it felt as if all the doors were opening up. It felt as if the city were receiving us with open arms. For the first month we stayed in a room at Shin's apartment, and by the second month we had found our own apartment in Crown Heights.

Sara was very fortunate and within a few weeks she found a job through a friend that was much better than her previous job, in both pay and fit. I was looking for jobs at the same time, and while I knew something would eventually align, my intuition struck again, this time with even stronger force. I felt a continuation of its original message, but now that I was in New York City, my intuition stated clearly that it wanted me to focus on writing. There may be moments when your intuition tells you something but you are too afraid to hear it. And that is OK. Just don't forget the message. Return to it when you feel ready. I had felt this call about a year before, but at the time I had not taken it seriously. It felt real and strong but also too different and new to me. This time it hit like lightning. I could feel that if I focused on writing now, it could be a good way to serve. I was already so impressed that healing was possible, and I wanted other people to know that it was available to them, too. They didn't need to do what I did, but, if they found their own way and methods, they could alleviate the tension in their mind and cultivate a better life.

To be honest, at first I was scared about what this would mean for our financial security, and I also felt uncomfortable about putting all this on Sara. Neither one of us comes from a wealthy family, and we were still very much living paycheck to paycheck. For days I wondered if pursuing a writing career was a real possibility. In fact, the idea of writing was so deeply covered up by thick conditioning that it had only revealed itself once I started meditating. It was a surprise when it came up to the surface. Eventually, after looking for jobs for a while, I gathered the courage to speak to Sara and bring her in to what I was considering. I asked her if she could give me some time to work on writing to figure out whether or not I could really do this.

I remember being so scared having that conversation with her, and while she definitely felt hesitation, she listened and agreed to give me a chance. I shared her nervousness as I was far from confident that I could make a career from writing. I had virtually no experience outside of essays for high school and college, but my intuition was very clear that it wanted me to spend time practicing, to spend time reading not just for pleasure but with an eye to learning the craft and to developing a voice of my own.

My Instagram account felt like a natural writing outlet. Being able to receive immediate feedback on the essays and small poems I was sharing helped me hone my writing so that I could reach people better. It was a long process, and most of that time I felt that I was failing. I was full of doubt and worried that I was messing up my chance at having a more traditional career, but I was determined to stick it out. For the next two years I spent a lot of time alone in our apartment, working on writing and focusing on finding my voice. Slowly, more and more people began reading and following me online. I was surprised and grateful that my words were resonating with readers. At a certain point, I felt confident enough to release a self-published version of my first book, *Inward*, and soon it was picked up by a publisher and distributed around the world. It feels like a miracle to this day, and I still find it hard to believe that taking that huge leap into writing actually worked. It would not have been possible if I had not had the courage to listen to my intuition. Even though I had nothing when I started, my intuition helped me build a vision and get on the right path.

The beauty of intuition is that, if you listen, it will push you to grow. In my experience, following what was clear in my gut made me address deeper and deeper levels of fear. It also pushed me to finally address my aversion to accepting help from loved ones. It taught me to have faith in the process, even though the plan was not crystal clear. Becoming a writer was always second to my personal growth and I had to realize that again and again as I was honing my written voice. Personal growth allowed me to discover this side of myself and it helped me access my creativity. This, in turn, helped me see that healing should always be my top priority. My creative ventures should come second because if my growth doesn't take precedence then all the work I do will be weakened by my loss of focus.

Emotional Maturity Is Having a Flexible Sense of Identity

When we think about healing, there is often this idea that we want to go back to being who we were before the hurt and trauma. On the surface, it may seem that healing is bringing us back to an original state, but when we take a deeper look, it is clear that who we are is always changing. The interaction between mental and physical phenomena occurs at incredible speeds—at the conventional level of everyday life, we may seem solid, but, in reality, our being is in a constant state of motion. This means that who we were in the past only remains as a memory; that person is not someone we can truly go back to.

Life flows forward, from one moment to the next. Though the present moment is similar to the most recent past moment, they are not fundamentally the same. Similarly, when we embrace our evolution and put energy into our transformation, we are giving a clearer direction to the flow of innate change that is happening within us. We reclaim our power by understanding our past and by intentionally living our present—this helps us build our future by choosing to make wise actions today.

A stagnant sense of identity can make life harder. Seeing your sense of self as something that never changes goes against the natural river of change that moves through existence. Allowing yourself the space for transformation—to build new habits, to develop new ideas or perspectives, to let go of old ways of being—will support you as you move through the ups and downs of life. An identity that is flexible will encourage your flourishing and support you in discovering new parts of yourself. Attempting to stay the same, or to get back to an old version of yourself, is a form of attachment that brings little security and causes much mental tension. If everything in existence is powered by change, our only option is to embrace it and let its movement inspire our evolution.

Accepting Difficult Moments

The best you is not the one who lives through easy times. The best you comes into being during and after great challenges. Hard moments give us the opportunity to apply the healing that we have accomplished so far and they fuel us to evolve even further. Challenges expand our capacity in ways that easy times do not, as they help us see how we have grown and in what ways we need to continue growing.

Too often, we think of healing in an external sense—we try to remove the obstacles from our lives without realizing that to make our healing long-lasting, it is more effective to address our own perception and reactions. There is nothing wrong with saying no to difficult people and putting ourselves on a better path that more substantially supports our happiness, but it would be unrealistic to expect that we can remove all difficulties from our lives. The ocean of life flows between calmness and storms. Honoring the truth that challenging moments are common will help us let go of resistance so that we can pass through difficult times with less tension and use them to gain more wisdom. Facing difficult situations head-on from a place of balanced action, rather than with blind reaction, is a sign of emerging emotional maturity.

Emotional maturity will manifest in greater amounts when we turn deeply inward to address all that has been left unprocessed from our emotional history. Emotional maturity brings a bounty of good things to our personal lives, but it also prepares us to create deeper relationships.

Reflections

In what ways has your emotional maturity flourished over the last few months? What are you able to do now that you weren't able to do before?

Are there instances you remember when you would try to run away from hard feelings or situations? What were they?

How has your self-awareness affected your emotional maturity? What does it feel like to be able to see more of yourself?

What is your relationship with your emotions these days? Are you able to honor and be with them when they arise?

In what ways would you like to develop your emotional maturity next?

Do you expect perfection from yourself? Are you able to let it go when you realize that you're demanding way too much from yourself?

Are you dealing with tough things from a place of peace or from a place of past hurt?

Have you found your middle path?

Chapter 7

Relationships

Love has many synonyms, including *mental clarity, compassion, selflessness, flexibility, attention, acceptance*, and *understanding*. It is so powerful because it is simultaneously hardy and elastic, like water. Love takes on the form it needs to bind people together in a wholesome and nourishing manner. But human beings are complex, and we carry the baggage of survivalist tendencies that we gathered during tough times. Love is freedom, while attachment is control—and all human beings enter relationships as a mix of both.

Love is interrupted by the pain we carry. It is easy to blame love itself for the hurt we feel, but all love does is open us up. The hurt comes from the heavy conditioning and ill-fated patterns that stop us from showing up in a compassionate manner. A person can be in love and also unprepared to care for that love. One can feel love for another but also have a variety of attachments that block their appreciation for the amazing connection that is right in front of them. Attachments, our cravings to have things exist in a very particular way, are the rocks that clog up the mighty flow of love. Our attachments are often molded by the hurt we have felt in the past. In this sense, attachments represent our inflexibility. Attachment has a self-centered approach to love, where you focus too much on how you want your partner to make you feel and not enough on treating them well. Connection has more room for balance, where you both seek to support each other's happiness and focus on communicating to find a good middle path, instead of trying to control each other. If a person can only focus on getting their preferred outcome, even at the cost of their partner's happiness, that means their mind is dominated by attachments. If someone only cares about how you make them feel and puts little effort into finding a middle ground where you are both giving and receiving support, this is an unhealthy connection. Real love feeds connection, not attachment.

What makes relationships work, even when we ourselves are so imperfect, is self-awareness. To be able to see inside yourself, to pay close enough attention to your mental movements that unconscious tendencies slowly become clear, is an act of love for yourself and for those around you. When you can see if you are being motivated by love or by attachment, you reclaim your power from habitual reactions and start utilizing your intention to bring more harmony into your responses. It takes self-awareness to choose love.

Love invites healing. It creates a path for two people not

only to blossom in self-awareness but to develop their emotional maturity. Love is a powerful light. If you are immersed in it and ready to grow, it will show you more of yourself. Love is not just for soothing you; it is an engine of evolution. Putting in effort to remove the reins of the past from your mind so that you can arrive at the present as an unburdened human being is a powerful act of love.

The greatest gift partners can give each other is a continuous commitment to their own personal healing. The love you are able to give to yourself and your partner is determined by your self-awareness. If your self-awareness is growing, you will have a greater capacity for intentional actions that are authentic. If you both find methods to help you unload the past that you carry, you will find your minds are lighter and there will be more space for you to deepen your connection. Love is a dynamic force, and if you are both able to loosen your attachments, you will flow together with greater ease.

The uncomfortable truth is that many who have never ventured into healing will struggle to love well. Those who do take their healing seriously have a greater chance at figuring out healthy ways of supporting each other's happiness. To build the type of home where both of you feel the spaciousness of freedom and the comforting support of the voluntary commitments you have made to each other is a goal worth pursuing.

●

we allow ourselves to love because it's worth the risk
even though there is the chance of loss or hurt
we take the leap again and again
because love is one of the best parts of being alive
we don't do it because it's easy
we do it because connection makes everything brighter

After Heartbreak

Breakups leave such a deep mark. The pain they cause ripples through our being and is a deep source of distress. The end of a relationship is the end of a home. Putting so much of your love, emotional energy, and effort into building a space that holds the two of you well is something deeply sacred. When it comes to an end, it is no surprise that we feel such deep sorrow. That sorrow then goes on to mold what we look for in future relationships and how we behave once we are in them. Often, this takes shape as having trouble opening up again, for fear of being hurt in the same way, or lack of confidence and feelings of unworthiness. Heartbreak and endings always point to how valuable self-love really is. When self-love is missing from within us, it will negatively affect our connections.

If we empower the love that already exists within us, it can flourish and make us feel much more whole than partnership ever can. True wholeness comes from within us. The heartache period is a reflective one, and one of its gifts is that it can show us what we are missing. And if we are honest with ourselves, not only can it activate self-love, but it can propel our growth by highlighting parts of our character that would benefit from positive cultivation. Examine how you can be a little more selfless, more understanding, a better listener, and not so attached or controlling. This will be exceptionally helpful as you move forward and this kind of self-examination is something courageous people do all the time.

Part of the love that we need to cultivate within ourselves is accepting the hard truths about where we went wrong. What patterns do we still hold that need addressing, and how should we behave next when another connection comes along? We also need to examine what we are looking for in a partner. Beauty is so incredibly fleeting that we need to make sure that we are also looking for qualities that would fit well alongside our own. Seeking someone who complements you with their own level of emotional maturity, willingness to grow, kindness, and honesty is key.

The feeling of being complete and no longer alienated from yourself cannot really come from another person's love or approval, though it may bring a fleeting sense of satisfaction. It is nowhere near as powerful as you cementing within yourself a profound sense of self-acceptance. *The only way loneliness will ever end is if you are no longer far away from yourself.* The distance that many of us have within is closed by being completely honest and bringing the peace of self-acceptance to each part of ourselves and our story. When we are no longer at war with ourselves, our self-love begins to blossom. If you take the time to know and love yourself deeply, you will become profoundly fulfilled, and this, in turn, will make all your connections much deeper and more fruitful.

One of the most valuable openings that heartbreak can create is realizing what type of qualities you want in a partner. Just because a connection is there doesn't mean there is enough emotional preparedness to build a nourishing partnership. Even though no one is perfect, being open to someone with a base of emotional maturity as you cultivate your own will increase your chances of connecting more deeply next time. Your emotional energy is sacred, and there is nothing wrong with treating it as such. If connection is what you are looking for, give your emotional energy to a person who is ready to cherish it and give their own.

Self-love is a matter of self-worth that brings balance to every connection we enter into. When we build a home within ourselves, furnished with emotional maturity and constructed on a foundation of self-awareness, we are actually setting ourselves up for future success whenever we decide to open our heart again to another person. Love is so attractive that even the pain of unwanted endings will eventually yield to the possibility that we may find the right connection with someone who is also ready for the type of love that goes deeper than the surface level—a love that welcomes growth and vulnerability. Even when it feels incredibly difficult to open up our hearts to such a sensitive depth, we still take the leap forward when our intuition makes it clear that we should try again.

People are quite different: Some people love being alone, while others desire a partner. But in each case there are still many connections in your life that will benefit directly from having a healthy relationship with yourself. Love exists in every human being, but the ways you show it depend on your conditioning and preferences. What matters most is that you tend to the love that dwells within you so that you can use it as a light as you travel through life.

●

there is no shortage of people who
you will find physically beautiful
but finding someone who matches
the maturity you are looking for
the dedication to grow
the humor that brings you comfort
and someone who just feels right in your arms
and life is incredibly unique

Your Healing Elevates the Relationship

If you allow the blocks within you to remain as they are and the wounds you carry to fester, then it will become easy to fall into a cycle where you are always looking for external validation. And that same lack of self-awareness will make it easy to constantly project the roughness that you feel onto others, especially those closest to you. Self-love is the missing piece in many relationships. This is why some of the most beautiful relationships develop over time and are spurred into evolution when both people realize that they have a lot to heal within themselves.

Even if the connection is strong, there still needs to be plenty of intentional time for the both of you to learn each other's preferences as well as get a good sense of how your emotional history, traumas, and aspirations affect the way you both show up in your relationship. Even when the love between you flows easily, there will still be hurdles to overcome. Love opens the door to vulnerability, which will allow more of each of you to come to the surface. The welcoming of this vulnerability sheds further light on the patterns you each carry, the fears you are working on overcoming, and the deep hurt that you each have unconsciously carried throughout your lives. Open hearts need tender care and, though you both welcome vulnerability, it will take knowing each other well to learn how to properly hold space during these moments of healing revelation.

Since healing is the cultivation of harmony within the individual, there is a direct connection between the depth of your healing and your ability to navigate the ups and downs of a relationship. A perfect stream of happiness, joy, and unending fun is not possible between two people. Your imperfections, ego, and survivalist habit patterns will occasionally cause ruptures that create friction in your relationship. The outside world will also pose difficulties you will need to navigate and adapt to. But if handled skillfully these challenges can bring you two even closer than before by building trust and understanding.

One of the best ways to get to know yourself is through interactions with other human beings. Silent meditation retreats or deep one-on-one sessions with a therapist are extremely productive, but putting the skills you've developed into action in the real world builds self-awareness in a whole new way. Intimate relationships take those interactions to another level because you mutually decide to build a bond. Together, you take on the adventure of building a home where you both feel safe, free, and nourished.

The profound proximity of relationships makes them excellent incubators for personal growth. To be in each other's presence not only allows you to practice love but also forces the ego to see itself, even if what you find is hard to bear. Proximity among imperfect human beings, even when they have cultivated a lot of emotional maturity and taken their inner work seriously, will eventually lead to some sort of discord or conflict. Try to look at these moments as opportunities for you both to see yourselves more clearly—moments when harmony has decayed so that it can be rebuilt with a wiser design.

Whether due to hardened old patterns that get in the way of loving each other right or a lack of self-awareness that doesn't let you see when you are projecting your emotions, unjustified blame and displaced anger are common when we are unaware of our mental movements. Relationships are often situations where the love is clearly there, but what makes them hard is all the emotional weight you have been carrying with you that slows the flow of clear observation and the compassionate support of each other's happiness. When your mind is burdened with tumultuousness and unresolved pain, the people around you will be impacted by your inner struggles. Even if you try to forget those struggles, what goes unprocessed will reveal itself in your actions, words, and thoughts. If you let your past rule you, it will be difficult to love others well in the present.

My wife, Sara, and I first met at Wesleyan University. She was an incoming freshman and I was a sophomore and the residential adviser on her floor. We pretty quickly found friendship in each other and would talk for long hours into the night. While the immediate connection between us was quite strong and undeniable, neither of us thought about becoming more than friends until a few months later, when I realized I was developing deeper feelings for her. Interestingly, our friends thought we were already a couple because we spent so much time together, but the truth was that we just kept seeking each other out to share more of our life stories. Even so, I was incredibly nervous about talking to her about the new feelings I felt for her.

I also noticed that I wasn't the only guy seeking her attention, so I was unsure if she even thought of me as more than a friend. But one night in early November I gathered the courage to finally tell her. I knew from our time together that she hadn't been in a relationship before, and I was probably more than a little excited when I was finally able to tell her my feelings, but I was still caught by surprise when her first reaction was to say she needed space to think about all this. Later that night, she told me she was ready to talk, but the first thing she said when we met up was, "What are you thinking long term?" I was so confused by her question that I blurted out, "Do you even like me?" Fortunately, she did, but she hadn't wanted to risk our friendship for a short fling (we laugh about that moment to this day).

We said we loved each other only a few weeks later. It just slipped out. But we had absolutely no idea how to build a healthy relationship together. Between the two of us, there was a grand total of zero emotional maturity. We would argue often, constantly swaying between the two extremes of being wildly in love and blaming each other for the inner pain we did not know how to manage. Even though we talked a lot, we communicated poorly. Our fights were drawn out because we both focused on winning. Neither of us had the patience to be the bigger person.

For years, neither of us could fully see, let alone communicate to the other, how so much of the friction between us was caused by the unobserved and unresolved tension that dwelled in us as individuals. Because we both lacked self-awareness, we had trouble seeing each other clearly. Even though we were together for years, there was always a distance between us. A lot of that was due to how dishonest I was being with myself about the sadness and anxiety that would periodically roar through my mind and push me further into reinforcing unhealthy habits. We both desired control in different ways and blamed each other for things that were unreasonable. The first six years of our relationship felt like we were moving in and out of a hurricane together. Many times we almost called it quits, and sometimes a breakup got incredibly close, but the connection between us kept us coming back. Today, I am so grateful that we kept trying. Now we feel very fortunate that we met so young and have gotten to be together for so long, but it was the healing work that we both undertook that saved our relationship and made it the pillar of strength that it is now in our lives.

It wasn't until we both started meditating that things really changed. Interestingly, we were each drawn to the same style of meditation and still find it fits our individual conditioning so well. We both began seeing that our relationship with ourselves as individuals was a total mess and that a lot of our behavior was not authentic at all. Much of it was composed of reactions driven by past trauma or intense emotions that we had accumulated over time. All these blind habit patterns were getting in the way of loving each other well.

Meditation has this critical ability to build self-awareness, which helped us notice when we were blaming each other for things that actually had nothing to do with the other. Slowly, we both started noticing how our inner tension would try to push us into bending logic to find a way to make it the other one's fault. Granted, sometimes we would certainly make mistakes that irritated each other, but many times we would look to make some trouble while our moods were low. Slowly, the constant finger pointing turned into "I want you to know that I don't feel good right now," which is a cue for the other that we could use support and compassion at the moment.

There were essential qualities that meditation cultivated in our separate minds. We both started enhancing our ability not to get pulled into immediate reactive impulses, to watch the rush of emotion, rather than getting dragged into it and making problems worse than they already were. The ability to pause and respond, instead of immediately reacting, was strengthened over time through our meditation, which taught us to observe the fire without giving it more fuel to burn.

We both began understanding ourselves better. We came

to deeply know what we wanted out of life, what we aspired to, how our past was affecting our present, and how our old conditioning clouded our ability to be fully receptive to each other. We saw our fears and learned how it was much more valuable to sit with them than to try to bury them or run away from them. We learned how, if we wanted to build freedom in our mind, we would have to take the route of honesty. We saw how the harshness in our minds stopped us from being gentle with each other in real life. The connection between what was happening in our minds and how we treated each other became shockingly clear. But this also gave us hope, because as our minds become less dense, patience, love, and selflessness were able to flow more easily between the two of us.

For the both of us, the first two years of meditating were a period of self-discovery and strong determination. We knew that the healing happening in our minds was bringing great results because we both felt much less tense, but we also knew that we had to remain committed to the practice to be able to fully benefit from the process. We started off by going to retreats, but over time we realized that it would benefit us immensely to start meditating daily at home. It felt like a herculean effort to push against the mix of laziness and the feeling of being too busy to make room in our lives for daily meditation. It made sense to do this because investing in the health of our minds was going to bring more harmony into our lives, but even that clear logic did not make sitting on the cushion easier. Eventually, we put our feet down and decided that, no matter what, we were going to move in this direction. Nothing was going to stop us.

Each couple has their own story, their own methods for overcoming the hurdles that relationships normally face. Recently, I reconnected with two good friends I originally met at Wesleyan; they have been together for about as long as Sara and I have. Over dinner we caught up about the general things you normally do, but I didn't want to miss this opportunity to find out if they had any wisdom to share about staying happy together. I said, "I know this is a big question and probably better for me to ask you separately, but how is your relationship going?" They smiled at each other and opened up about their truth. They had only recently moved in together after years of living in different cities. The pandemic spurred them to take the leap. But it wasn't easy at first; they didn't have much experience dealing with each other outside of short visits, during which they mainly focused on fun and light connection. If one of them felt down during those days, they would feel bad about it because they wanted to keep things joyous for the limited time they had together. They quickly discovered after they moved in together that they had been staying away from big topics they needed to address. Fortunately, they didn't wait to see if things would "just work themselves out" and sought the help of a relationship therapist. They laughed, describing the journey of trying to find the right therapist, but eventually they found someone they both felt comfortable working with. The therapist helped them get out of old patterns and address the issues that stood in the way of loving each other well.

They told me about one particular pattern that had left a big mark: They had been unconsciously holding on to their idea of each other from when they first met. In their minds, they would see each other as their younger versions in college, but this was becoming a hindrance in their relationship because they had grown up and changed in deep ways. They learned that they have to be intentional about loving the person who is in front of them now. Those old images they carried of each other did not include the multitude of lessons, wisdom, and personal healing gathered over the many years since they had first met. They were new people, but still in love—a deeper and more mature love. Finally, they started connecting with the person in front of them, instead of an outdated version that only existed in the past.

I was so happy for them because the strength of their connection was evident and their commitment to growth had added so much more to their relationship. They both felt fresh and so comfortable in each other's presence. They even talked about possibly seeing their therapist a few more times to be proactive about their relationship, even though the love was flowing now and a new level of harmony had been reached. They said their experience with the couples therapist was so worthwhile that they believed they would gain more valuable insight from her to help them keep deepening and upgrading their connection.

Good Communication Makes a Difference

Couples are strikingly different, and the way your relationship story will unfold is unique to you. But even though relationships are complex and situational, it is still possible to build systems that meet your relationship where it is. Perhaps it is through meditation or a couples therapist, or another method entirely, but it's so worth the effort to find the tool that works for the two of you to build harmony and self-awareness.

A key element in developing a harmonious relationship is establishing a framework of communication that will help you both handle down moments. You need to think about what to do when one of you feels down and how to handle conflict between the two of you whenever it arises.

When one of you feels down, it is essential to communicate this clearly to your partner. Letting them know where you are on your emotional spectrum will give both of you the knowledge you need to handle this moment peacefully and successfully. For the person who feels down, naming the feeling helps bring it out into the open so that there is no confusion and so they don't need to act like they are happier than they actually are. When your self-awareness embraces the reality of this tough moment, you can then lean on treating yourself gently as the storm passes. Accepting where you stand within yourself helps you prevent these temporary tough emotions from trying to bend logic and create conflict where there is none.

Admitting out loud that our mood is down can sometimes be difficult because we are revealing our imperfections and vulnerabilities. But often this act helps to break the downward mental spiral. Sometimes our tough moods have a clear cause, like something from the past that was triggered, but other times our emotional shifts will not be so easily identifiable. It is just like waking up in the morning— sometimes you wake up with sadness or some sort of mental heaviness, and other times you spring up out of bed, ready to put your best foot forward and take on the day. Whether or not you know the cause, how you embrace the reality within you and manage your reactions so that they don't become worse is up to you. Your power is in how you respond to the mental situation confronting you.

Sara and I have worked out a system for supporting each other during tough emotional moments. We let each other know when our emotions feel turbulent by saying, "Anger has come up" or "I have a lot of anxiety moving through me," instead of saying, "I am angry" or "I am anxious." Saying it in this way reaffirms that our identity is separate from this temporary emotion. The next part of our system is that the one who is feeling more balanced takes the lead in terms of supporting the other. When one of us is feeling down, the other will try to take something off their plate by cooking dinner, cleaning up, or doing any other busywork that may feel like too much to handle that day. We try to step up and support each other, because even though storms are temporary, they can be quite unsettling as they move through a person. We've found that being asked for support is preferable to receiving misdirected blame or tension. Asking your partner to hold space for you as you face what is happening inside you can help you smoothly navigate the storm and minimize any friction that arises when you encounter a hard moment.

When people are in close proximity, there is bound to be some conflict, but emotionally mature individuals will try to use conflict as an opportunity to build understanding and develop deeper harmony. No relationship is perfect because no individual is perfect. Conflict is natural because we all carry egos that are normally more motivated by craving than by honesty. When conflict arises, it is not a sign that something is fundamentally wrong, and it is not necessarily a bad thing. If it is handled wisely, it can help you both know yourselves more deeply and honor your truths while remaining flexible. Conflict should not be seen as something that should never happen—in fact, it is bound to happen, so you might as well learn to navigate it skillfully.

Whenever conflict arises between the two of you, the most essential thing to keep in mind is that managing problems is not about winning. If both of you keep trying to win the argument, both of you will lose. Ego craves to win, but loving clarity seeks to understand. When you bring awareness to your ego, it loses its power and gives more space for your actions to become motivated by compassion. *When you both let go of winning, what is left is doing your best to understand each other.* To see each other clearly, you need to take turns sharing your perspective. When one is sharing their perspective, the other needs to do their best to listen selflessly. This is sometimes a very hard task, especially if your emotions are wrapped up in the situation. But if you both give each other the consideration of realizing that the other person's perspective is valid and that it actually does not negate your own perspective, it will help defuse the situation so you can wholeheartedly hear their point of view and try to place yourself in their shoes. This only works if you both take turns and seriously accept the task of listening openly and calmly.

Selfless listening does require some degree of emotional maturity—the ability to feel your truth but not be totally dominated by it, so you can grasp more of what's happening than just your immediate emotions. When it is time for you to share your perspective, it is most helpful to describe things from your point of view, without being accusatory or defensive. Focus on describing how something made you feel and how you would have preferred for things to transpire. If you realize that you did do something wrong, own it openly and take responsibility for it. This does not give up your power; it is a powerful tool to defuse an argument. If this is a situation where both of you did something to agitate the other, then it is best to have the humility to own your part and apologize for it.

What Does Supporting Each Other's Happiness Really Mean?

Giving support sometimes feels like a vague term because the support we need as individuals is so situational. What we need may change from one day to the next and certainly from one year to another. But there are some clear essentials about giving proper support that can help us navigate this critical aspect of healthy relationships.

Understand that another person cannot make you happy. This is often one of the hardest pills to swallow. Society has deeply conditioned us to expect that happiness will be ours once we get in the right relationship. We're told that our partner will be able to bring everything that has been missing in our lives, that one person can fulfill all our needs and cravings and bring us limitless joy. The truth is that these are unhealthy expectations that are based on a strong attachment to pleasure. We have no option but to take responsibility for our own happiness. Happiness has to be cultivated from the inside out. Your mental state gives color and vibrancy to your external environment. You can have a calm life and a wonderful partner and still be unhappy if you have not properly assessed your internal landscape.

Understand that another person cannot fix your emotional problems. On a similar note, we often expect our partners to be the answer for our own internal turbulence. We think the love they give us will be enough to bring lasting peace to our minds and erase the hard past that affects us on a daily basis. Avoiding responsibility, doing nothing to understand your own story, and not trying to manage your reactions will create conflict in your relationship. If you do not understand that your emotional stability rests on your own shoulders, it becomes easy to fall into a loop where you blame your partner for inner tension that arises within you, even when that tension is not necessarily related to them.

Recognize that healthy support has to be mutual. Both of you should be doing your best to be there when the other needs it. It takes two people giving active support to create a harmonious relationship. If only one person is in a constant state of giving and the other is always receiving without ever doing their part, the partnership will quickly become exhausting. Partnerships should be a space of growth and rejuvenation. It is more than likely that both people entering the relationship will still have much to learn about themselves and what it takes to create long-lasting love, but this is where communication becomes critical. Letting each other know how you need support gives the other person a chance to put forward effort, even if giving active support is something new for them. None of us will get it right every single time, but noticeable effort will make a substantial difference.

Avoid coercion and manipulation. Supporting each other's happiness has to be voluntary if there is to be real unity between the two of you. Our emotional capacities are quite different, and so are our strengths, as well as the ways we show and prefer to receive love. Demanding a very specific form of support can backfire if it does not feel healthy for the other person to show up in the way you are asking. Ultimately, we can ask for support, but we cannot corner or coerce one another to get what we want. That isn't real love and it is potentially harmful. What is possible is patiently sharing how you would each like to be supported and checking within yourselves to see if these are ways that you can show up for each other. The key is to find a match between ways your partner is looking for support and what feels possible within the realm of your emotional range. If they are asking for something that is not doable for you, honor yourself by saying so.

Flexibility. The last critical piece is flexibility. Whether or not we are open to growth, all of us are constantly changing beings. What works one day may not help us in a new situation. When you both lean on active communication and check in on what helpful support looks like for each of you, you are setting yourselves up for success. Guessing games are a recipe for disaster, so never expect your partner to be able to read your mind. You are better off being vocal about where you are and what you need so that the one you love can come forward to support you. Seeing each other as changing beings who will naturally have shifting preferences over time will make it easier to switch things up whenever necessary.

Sara and I are always working on our relationship, but one thing I do think we have both been aware of since we started intentionally growing as individuals is not demanding that it be perfect. Demanding perfection from a relationship will crush it out of existence. Coming into equilibrium with this understanding and realizing that a relationship is the ultimate practice in sharing (you share your life, your joy, the hard parts, and the victories) will help you cultivate the right amount of selflessness to assist the relationship on its own journey of growth and evolution. Even though you are each individuals, you do not exist as silos—you open yourselves enough so that your loving bond can also hold you both as one. Your union essentially has three major components: you, your partner, and your actual relationship. And all three must be fed, nourished, and cultivated for harmony to flow with greater ease.

You should each get at least half of what you want. But the half that you get does not remain static. It should change over time and reflect the things that are actually important to you. This may include the ways you like your partner to support your happiness, how much time you generally spend together, and other major decisions that affect both of you. Through clear communication, you can both specify not just what actually matters to you when you are setting up the emotional design of your home, but more mundane everyday decisions, like what to eat or watch together on TV. You may ask yourself, If I am only getting half of what I want, could I really be happy? Is this even realistic? Since you are two sovereign beings, there is no other fair option but to share leadership; if one person is deciding everything in the relationship, this can quickly devolve into an unhealthy or even hurtful pattern. This is not to say that each individual won't have different strengths in decision making. Sara is really good at making everyday decisions, like organizing the daily tasks that we need to accomplish, while I excel at long-term decisions, like knowing when it is time to make a big move or planning for our future. I am inclined toward taking risks and she is risk-averse. Understanding that about each other helps us land in the middle so that we both feel comfortable about major decisions we make. Of course we get input from each other on all joint decisions, and we discuss things thoroughly. Relationships work when you intentionally try to share control. In situations where one person is adamant about always getting what they want, this is automatically unhealthy. At best you can each control half the relationship, but not all of it.

If you only get half of what you want, know that the other half is not lost. Rather, you get the other half in feeling sympathetic joy for your partner's happiness in getting what they want. If this is a person you truly love, you will want to support them in honoring their power and being happy. There is a high likelihood that you will get much more than half of what you want because you and your partner's interests will align in many different cases. If you truly love them, you will feel joy when they get what they want.

Deeper Into Communication

Miscommunication between two people is incredibly common because every time someone speaks they are translating their feelings into words, and then the other person has to interpret those words through the filter of their own current feelings and past emotional history. Since we are communicating through filters of perception, it takes a certain degree of calmness and emotional maturity between two people to ask each other, "What do you mean by this?" or "Can you tell me more?" to really understand what is being said. Communication without patience is likely to turn into conflict. Communication with patience is likely to lead to deeper connection.

The power of communication in a relationship cannot be overstated. It is the bedrock of your union and its savior during challenging moments. Communication is how you keep each other informed regarding your individual truths and any changes that have occurred in your needs. Especially in the beginning of a relationship, you are better off communicating frequently and erring on the side of overcommunicating until you both develop a better understanding of each other. With openness and time, you will learn more about each other's longstanding preferences. Even if you have been together for decades, you will not be able to read each other's minds, and since you are both beings of change, there will still be new opinions, ideas, and stories to share with each other. Listening to each other with a selfless mindset— one where you let go of your own view for a moment so that you can compassionately examine your partner's view—will help you both build a much deeper understanding of how you each experience things.

the real game changer is when you stop
making assumptions about what your partner
is saying and simply ask them for clarification
this can prevent false narratives
that cause arguments from sneaking into your mind
and save your feelings from getting hurt

If you can take turns practicing selfless listening, it will help both of you feel that your reality is being heard. Healthy modes of communication, based on compassionate honesty and selfless listening, create a deeper level of respect between the two of you. Even though perspectives may be cloudy because of everything each of you has gone through in the past, there is still a lot of value in honoring the fact that even a cloudy perspective can have real implications for how you feel. All humans want to be seen. If you can give that gift to your partner, it will build an incredible amount of trust and unity.

The type of communication that brings two people close together cannot occur without honesty. It is easy to fall into cycles of white lies as a means of people-pleasing or to avoid conflict, but even small lies create distance. To reach deeper levels of love and unity, you have to take the path of honesty with yourself and those around you. If you really want to *be* with someone, it means there is no more space for running or lying. A synonym for *love* is *truth*.

The reality is that you are going to make mistakes and neither of you will get it right all of the time. Being in a mature relationship is not about perfection; it is about embracing the fact that you are both in the midst of growth, which makes communication even more important. What brings you together is not just the love you have but the commitments you have both willingly made to help your relationship thrive.

maturity is being able to maintain
your energy the way you want it to be
when someone close to you is trying to
drag you into their storm

you hear them
you offer support
but at the same time
you let their tension be theirs
and you let your peace be yours

●

The Value of Friendship

Signs of a deep friend connection:

Laughter is abundant.

Honesty is encouraged.

Support is real and active.

Vulnerability is welcomed.

You can put your guard down.

You inspire each other to grow.

You give each other good advice.

Both of you feel stronger together.

You help each other weather storms.

Some of our greatest connections are with our chosen family. When we connect with the right people, it makes a massive difference. We make a lot of friends throughout our lives: Some are temporary, others last for a few years, and a select few will endure for decades or a lifetime. The friends who really stand out and leave their marks are those we can truly share our story with and who stand by us in stormy times. The intuitive click that makes us want to connect with someone often leads us to great people we are meant to share a part of our life with. You know the connection is real when you don't feel inclined to perform a false version of yourself. Real friends have a naturally disarming nature that helps us put our guard down and allow the most real version of ourselves to step forward.

There are some close friends we welcome hard truths from and no one else. Real friends don't offer blind support. Though it can be difficult to receive, it is a gift to have someone in your closest circle who isn't afraid to tell you when you are moving in the wrong direction. Not because they are projecting their fear onto you or because they want to control you, but because they genuinely care about your wellbeing. Since they know you deeply, they feel empowered to be radically authentic with you. They share words that help reignite your fire so you can get back on the right path when you waver. Above all, the friends who last are the ones who appreciate you as you grow, see the value of your healing, and support you as you undergo transformation. They don't appreciate you because you put on an act; they appreciate you because they love your realness.

I met my closest friend, Lennon, when I was in the fourth grade. It feels incredible that our bond has withstood so many different eras of our lives since then. We ended up in the same middle school and high school, and became especially close in those years. We were always getting into deep discussions about movies and books that we wanted to share and dissect with each other. When we were hanging out with other people, we often functioned as a team, playing off each other's jokes, introducing each other to different circles, and always being open to adventures and meeting new people. Even when I moved away to college, our connection stayed solid. I would make time to see Lennon on breaks and spent most of my summers at his house. Over the years I spent so much time at his mom's house that it felt like my second home. College, especially at first, was challenging for me. I was the first person in my family to go and it was all on me—applying, financial aid forms, standardized tests. Even my guidance counselor discouraged me from applying to Wesleyan, the school I ended up going to. The transition from a diverse city to a small college town was incredibly disorienting. Knowing I had my family and friends like Lennon back home helped enormously.

I felt lost again after I graduated from college and moved back home, but Lennon never left my side, even though my energy was pretty negative and agitated. He was searching for more at the time, too, looking for a better life, a more expansive identity. We supported each other as we figured things out. Our friendship was never perfect—we fought a bunch of times and made mistakes that hurt each other—but what kept us as close as brothers was that we would always talk things out. One thing I didn't want to run away from was our friendship. It felt too valuable to lose over something trivial or some absentminded mistakes. Even when we would hit long rough patches, we both still knew that we were there for each other, no matter what.

His mother, Ann, passed away recently and her death put things in perspective for me. Not having her around feels like something essential is missing in my life. I loved talking to her because she treated me like an adult, even when I was really young. I felt that she was always watching out for us, to make sure we were OK, but never in an overbearing way. In her absence, it feels like the responsibility for our lives is now fully on our own shoulders. The loss feels big for me, but for Lennon it is unimaginable. It showed me how close he and I really were because my heart roared with compassion for his loss. The day of his mother's memorial, we all shared pieces of her life and spoke about the impact she had on us. Lennon spent parts of the ceremony sitting between me and my mother. A bond like that transcends description. Today we keep in touch frequently, even though we no longer live in the same city.

What worked especially well for the two of us is that we set the expectations really low for each other. That may sound counterintuitive, but this degree of flexibility helped us with the ebb and flow of our friendship. Some years we didn't spend much time hanging out and others we would spend whole weeks together. The situation kept changing because life kept moving on, but we both maintained an unspoken open door policy. The other strength was that neither of us was afraid to talk through the rough moments, and, once the talking was done, we let it go and moved on. We were also there for each other when struggle would appear in our personal lives or when we needed to think things through with another person. We shared the different parts of our lives with each other. We both had different friend groups that did not overlap, but nothing felt exclusive and when the opportunity arose, we would introduce each other to our new friends. What kept everything open was that it was just so easy to talk to each other. Our past had a way of smoothing out any awkwardness, even if we had not seen each other in a long time.

Commitments can certainly be made in friendships, but they are different from those in an intimate relationship. You want your friends to be reliable, but they also need freedom to build their lives and process tough moments in ways that suit them best. The person you meet in one particular era of your life will not remain the same. Just as you need to focus on your own evolution, they need to do the same. Friends who support each other in growth have to find deeper things that connect them than something that is temporary or surface-level. Connecting on the level of values, views of the world, history together, and the intuitive pull to be around each other can help become a foundation for a long-lasting friendship. Laughter can bring you together, but it's what you share during authentic moments that makes a friendship truly feel like home.

The other side of things is that a great friendship doesn't need to last forever for it to be an incredibly profound part of your life story. Sometimes you overlap with a person for a specific purpose and you spend a lot of time together, but, as you both grow, life takes you in different directions. New interests emerge that set you on the path of new adventures. Even though your time together has ended, there is no real love lost. We only have so much time to give to other people, especially as we grow older. Priorities become clearer and sometimes that means sacrifices. Maintaining an active friendship takes energy and time, but even though we dearly love a person, it won't always be possible to spend all the time we wish we could together. We are human, and the amount of time we have for ourselves and others is finite.

Reflections

What aspects of old relationships are you committed to not repeating again?

How is your practice of listening selflessly going? Can you focus on the other person's words without immediately thinking about how you will respond?

How has your personal healing affected your relationship? Is it bringing up challenges or opening up doors for deeper connection?

What can your partner do to support your happiness?

What can you do to support your partner's happiness?

What system have you figured out that works well during arguments? Have you both shifted from trying to win to truly trying to understand each other?

How would you describe the level of communication between you and your partner or your closest friend?

Have you each taken ownership of your own happiness?

Have you succeeded in releasing unfair expectations of each other—for instance, expecting your partner to be perfect all the time or expecting your relationship to always be fun?

Chapter 8

Challenges during Healing

Healing is for the brave and for those ready to face what lies within. There is so much inside of us, depending on our personal emotional history, that at times it can feel overwhelming. What your journey looks like in the beginning will be sharply different from what it looks like once you are deep in the emotional trenches of inner discovery. The popular understanding that healing is not linear is totally correct. The deepest parts of healing come in waves and between the waves there are periods of integration so you can connect with the new you. Along the way the challenges will be unique to your conditioning and related to the method(s) you have picked to aid you in your quest of developing greater happiness. If letting go was easy, no one would be hurting. So it is no surprise that the process of letting go will be filled with ups and downs. But if you can handle them with awareness, openness, and a keen mind that is ready to learn more, the ups and downs will help fill you with new wisdom.

Measuring Your Progress during the Journey

A common challenge is trying to measure your progress while you are in the midst of the process. You don't want to judge yourself when you are feeling particularly stormy, as your perspective is clouded. Since so much of healing is dependent on the sharpness of our self-awareness, we do not always realize how we are training our mind to become like a microscope that magnifies the roots of all our mental patterns and movements. This focus on expanding what we are conscious of by turning our attention inward results in an influx of new information that helps us understand ourselves at a much deeper level.

Sometimes this new clarity is taken to an extreme when we see all our imperfections at once and try to measure our growth from a specific moment, instead of across the length of our journey. For example, we sometimes feel the need to compare how we are today with how we were yesterday, or how we are this month with how we were last month. Taking these really small sample sizes does not fully account for the fact that healing is not linear. During short periods of time, there may be a lot of back-and-forth movement, highs and lows, or new discoveries about ourselves that require us to slow down so we can fully integrate this new knowledge.

Or, we may simply have a lot of accumulated reactions from the past that have finally come up for release. Either way, our attachment to perfection will crave sharp upward progress, when the truth of the journey is much more complicated and unpredictable.

Granted, the purpose of even embarking on your healing journey and taking your evolution seriously is to come out as a better version of yourself. Still, it is critical to understand that, even though there is ultimately an upward trajectory, in the midst of that rise you will encounter the messy reality of undoing the old and practicing the new, which is bound to come with the constant stream of changes that occur in life.

If you really want to take a good look at yourself, this is best done in comparison to how you were before you even began all this inner work. Intentionally relaxing that microscopic self-awareness by taking a big step back to look at a bigger chunk of your life will give you a much better idea of how far you have come. A noticeable difference between how you are managing your reactions now and how you managed them in the past is a major sign of progress. If you react with less intensity than before and are able to choose more productive options that support your well-being and authenticity, you are on the right track.

This higher level of self-awareness is useful, but if we are not careful about when we use it and where we direct it, it can give us a skewed idea of the depth of our progress. It is especially important to suspend self-analysis during your

deepest down moments. When the mind is full of turbulence, it will not be easy to take a good look at yourself or to
engage in a balanced form of self-analysis. Being able to
recognize when you are in a serious down moment is itself a
sign of progress. So is suspending any harsh judgments
about where you are and quieting concerns about whether
your progress is real. Having that clear ability to feel where
you are as you travel through the spectrum of emotions will
help you transition from doing serious inner work to taking
it easy on yourself and treating yourself gently until the
storm passes.

Recognizing the down moment and using it as a signal to
embody patience toward yourself and others is a sign of
your growing wisdom. It will also help you refrain from
doing things you will later regret or getting into any illogical
arguments because your inner tension was pushing you to
fight. Focusing on moving gently through your day while
your mind goes through its storm is not a matter of being
fake or suppressing your emotions. It is a matter of honoring
a greater range of your reality. Yes, you don't feel great, but
you also understand that fueling this fire by adding tension
on top of your existing tension won't make anything better.
Your only beneficial option is to feel the heaviness of your
truth and not add any more weight to what your mind is
already working on releasing.

Similarly, you don't want to expect that every day will be
a triumph. Some days will be hard simply because healing is

a matter of fundamentally saying goodbye to the old you and your old ways of being. This will be challenging because you will be moving against the current of your old human habit and repeatedly trying to activate your human nature. In time, it will become easier to be the authentic you, but in the beginning it will feel as if you are constantly having to intentionally slow down to break an old pattern. It may feel tedious and tiring, and it will take a high level of commitment to unbind the knots that have been tying you down, but it will be tremendously worthwhile.

In reality, the journey is full of stumbles and some backtracking before a big leap forward. You will have to continuously address your attachment to perfection and to constant upward progress by recognizing it when it arises and remembering that this journey will not be a simple one. And it will be unique to your emotional history. The movement from the dark unknown to the glow of understanding will not be picture-perfect. So stay committed to your healing, but be gentle with yourself. When we take up the inner journey, we are accepting the challenge to evolve and flourish.

Moments of Tough Release

When we look inward, it has to be done with courage because what we find will often be jarring. Healing helps clean the mind, but first it will show you the patterns that cause you the most anguish. There are so many things that have been suppressed that when we take the time to explore our inner world, many old moments and rough emotions will come up for observation and release. The hard part of healing is that we have to be willing to face the storms if we are to enjoy the light of better days.

Even without active suppression, much is accumulated. When you react to especially strong emotions, they leave an imprint on the subconscious, which sets you up to feel that same emotion again when the mind perceives a similar situation. Unbinding these knotted-up burdens and unchaining ourselves from old conditioning sometimes causes moments of turbulence when the past comes alive within us, making the mind feel cloudy and dense as they pass through and finally exit our being.

When you are building self-awareness and intentionally trying to break out of old patterns, the past has a way of thundering into the forefront of your mind. The emotional reactions that have accumulated over time in the subconscious will rise up from the depths, temporarily shaking up your mind and making it cloudy and dark.

These down moments can be to your benefit if you manage them in a way that sets you up for present and future success. The down moments, when you feel old hurts again, are a new opportunity to process things in a healthy way, as opposed to repeating what didn't work in the past. Ultimately, down moments will keep happening, but you will know your healing is effective when you feel well equipped to handle them with gentleness and the patient understanding that no emotion in the history of your life has ever been permanent.

Times of deep release, when the debris of the past is cleansed from the mind, can make us feel weighed down for hours or even days. While these moments often feel like they are going to last forever, remind yourself that they are temporary. Breaking our allegiance to our past by saying no to old patterns and intentionally giving our energy to new positive habits can sometimes make us feel fear or doubt as we enter into a new era of our life, but recognizing these temporary moments as a shedding of the past and trusting the process can help us more wisely ride the ups and downs of healing.

The process of letting go is often quiet, but sometimes you will have to feel what you once rejected or tried to run away from for it to fully leave your being. Of course, the memories don't go away, but the emotional energy wrapped around certain memories or ideas is the obstacle that we have to train ourselves to dissipate. Even if past emotions roar as they are released, we do not need to roar back. We just need to let ourselves be with our truth—being with our truth becomes our means for healing.

It is easy to mistake a stormy moment for taking steps backward. However, these steps are laying the groundwork for taking a big leap forward. Storms serve two main purposes: They give you an opportunity to practice acceptance and gentleness *and* they help you release whatever is coming up. Whenever you are going deep, it is common to have off days, when you can't show up as the 100 percent best version of yourself. Healing will sometimes require you to focus more of your energy and attention internally so you can tend to the thick conditioning that is in the midst of being unbound.

When you feel a lot of agitation, you need to be aware that your mind will look for objects (people, ideas, or situations) to focus on so that it can further increase the agitation. Tension needs fuel to burn, and that fuel is normally the attachments that keep the mind from fully accepting the present moment as it is. A mind that is already caught in a storm tends to set aside rational and compassionate thinking. Passive aggressiveness and unnecessary conflicts are common when we let our mental heaviness chart the course of our actions. The mind is more familiar with turbulence than it is with peace. It tends to swing between mental images of the past and the future. Peace requires intentional mental training because it can only be found in the present moment.

If it ever gets too tough, that is a sign that you need to lean into your community—connect with friends or reach out to your therapist or meditation guide, whoever has been showing you how to navigate your internal world and move forward successfully on your journey. If they helped you open up, then they should be able to guide you through processing your old conditioning. The key is to move gently through the storm. Being with the agitation is more productive than adding to the agitation.

Having a circle of friends who can be your comrades on the healing journey can be an incredible support system. People who are engaging in a similar introspective method as you will have experienced similar ups and downs and will much more easily feel compassion for the struggles you are grappling with. Give people the opportunity to help and support you. You are giving others a chance to perform a wholesome and meritorious action by saying yes to the kindness and support they offer. Just as it is important to serve others, it is valuable to let others serve you. When we let others help us, we are actively letting go of the egocentric idea that we can handle everything on our own. Human beings are meant to live in community, which means finding a balance of giving and receiving within the social groups that we call home. When we help each other, we simultaneously practice selflessness and make our own futures brighter. Every action plants a seed that will later blossom and bring its fruit into our lives.

Unconsciously, we get attached to a linear idea of healing and progress. We expect there to be a constant trend of increasing peace, happiness, and bliss. But, truthfully, healing is more about building a profound and honest relationship with the truth you are feeling in the moment. Whether your mood is up or down you are encouraging yourself to be with whatever feels true for you.

Letting Go of the Old You

Another challenge during healing is to let go of the old you. As the deep work of release continues, your conditioning will become lighter and lighter. This will cause major shifts in what you like and don't like, and it will transform what you look for in connections. It is common to feel an inner struggle when you unconsciously try to hang on to your old self, because that is what you know best. We crave safe territory and fear the unknown. There is often an attachment to how you used to be, even if there were aspects of yourself that caused you a lot of tension. There may even be a push and pull regarding your perception when you struggle to allow yourself to see the world in a new way.

Since so much of your perception is governed by what you encountered in the past, it will feel simultaneously strange and refreshing to look at things and take them for what they are without constantly evaluating them according to what you remember. Focusing your perception on the present takes intentional action. Just as you had to do the work of letting go, you will have to accept the new you that is emerging and follow through with the positive habit building that supports your inner renaissance. If you are serious about your healing, you need to let your identity be flexible and flow in the direction that best supports your happiness.

Developing maturity in your healing journey means deeply embracing the fact that you will have to continuously let go of who you were, even within short periods of time. Who we are is constantly changing, but when we start giving the river of change a direction, the shifts we experience can become quite pronounced.

I always thought of myself as someone who loves and primarily reads history books. But as I kept meditating, new parts of myself would appear. I started developing a new love for other kinds of nonfiction books and literature, and my childhood love for science-fiction reemerged. Now I try to stay away from making a hard classification of what I like to read and instead just go with what intuitively feels right in the moment.

Allowing yourself to step forward in an organic manner that is always open to evolution helps align you with the natural flow of nature. Nature is always changing; nothing ever stands truly still. If you look deep enough, you will always find movement. This same principle is true about identity. Your being is in a state of perpetual motion. Nothing about you has ever been static, and even at your most subtle core there is the dynamic movement of change. In your everyday life, this will mean that the ways you understand yourself may fit for some time, but eventually you will need to discard these understandings and adopt new ones that make space for your growth.

The ego loves labels, not only for the sake of understanding but also to acquire more kindling for the fire of attachment. Labels function as brakes that help us counteract the natural flow of change, and sometimes they even serve as a form of resistance to doing healing work.

After periods of deep healing, labels that once seemed to help identify you may feel worn out. Understandings that once struck you with a sense of awe may also later feel like they lack complexity or depth. And as your wisdom expands, perspectives you hold about the universe may one day feel too limiting. Healing is a continuous state of growth. As we grow, we are bound to require refined and more subtle perspectives to help us understand the human condition. To avoid any unnecessary suffering, it serves us not to become attached to what we know, to understand that the views we hold may serve us temporarily, and to recognize that acquiring more experience and wisdom will set us up to let go of what we once thought was useful. Even in the span of one moment, what we know about ourselves and the world can change, especially if we remain open to the type of growth that helps us reclaim our power and enhance our happiness.

Even our relationship to our old hurts can become a hindrance if we see it as something static that we can never get rid of. If we identify too intensely with our trauma and it becomes a critical part of our identity, it may slow down our healing process because we may fear what life will be like without it. Growth itself is a process of creation and destruction. A new you is constantly being formed as the old you decays and becomes formless. Hanging on to the remnants of the past will only delay your arrival into the present. If you want to live in a way that supports your freedom, you have no other option but to let go.

We may at times feel odd when we outgrow the preferences that we were familiar with. We may even feel a little lost when we realize that we have outgrown our old life. In these moments, it helps to remind ourselves that it is fine to have new favorites, new ways of expressing ourselves, and new aspirations. To fully embrace growth, we must be willing to venture into the unknown.

Identity is tricky. You need it to have a frame of reference that helps you interact with the world, but too much identity and added labels will push you away from the truth of impermanence. Wisdom will welcome you to its home, but you have to disarm yourself before you enter. Wisdom will find you ready and worthy when you let go of all ideas and views. You can only enter when you are ready to observe yourself without judgment and without a perception that is hampered by the past. Understanding yourself is one thing, but timeless wisdom asks you to take a step further by letting go of everything.

Let go of who you thought you were and embrace the river of change flowing through every moving part that creates the perception of you: Only then will wisdom introduce you to freedom. Freedom flourishes in the field of ultimate reality, where the moving combinations of subatomic particles clearly demonstrate the insubstantiality of all human egos. Because we exist momentarily, how we define ourselves carries only a fleeting value. It is a good thing to know your-self, but it is even more worthwhile to free yourself. A lot of the unlearning that freedom requires involves peeling back the labels and layers that we once thought were the core of who we are to take on new labels and understandings of ourselves when necessary, but with the understanding that, in time, these will also change. You need a self to skillfully maneuver the world, but you need to completely let go of the self if you want to achieve ultimate liberation. Living in balance with these two truths gives you greater access to inner peace.

Being Okay with Slow Movement

One of the most toxic ideas that grips our minds is perfec-tion. We expect it, we crave it, we wish to see it in our lives and relationships, but reality and the idea of perfection are in a constant state of friction. Reality is ever-changing. It is transformation combined with unpredictability. Perfection is the opposite. It is an attempt to control and keep things within the boundaries of a certain mental image. Reality is a flowing river. Perfection is a static painting.

Especially when it comes to our personal growth and the quality of our relationships, perfection has a sneaky way of warping our perception so that great things seem less than they really are, and small problems seem unnecessarily large. Those of us who wish to live a good life not only need to have the humility to question our perception, but we should also periodically check in with ourselves to see if perfection has created tension by taking the reins of our mind.

Much of life's harmony emerges when we let go. If we can take our goals and work toward them by embracing progress, instead of aiming for perfection, we will build a sturdy foundation for long-lasting change. We do not need to rush to be productive. Practicing slow movement will not only decrease inner turmoil; it can also make us more effective.

Slow movements are intentional, powerful, and intelligently considered. To boldly move at our own pace and remove ourselves from any self-imposed competition can be a profound paradigm shift. Setting aside rigid time lines, embracing organic development, and maintaining focus on deliberate actions can make an immense difference in how much we achieve. In the equation for inner and outer success, speed is a small factor. We are better off concentrating on effort, commitment, and long-term consistency. Remember: Part of what makes mountains so mighty and enduring is that they are built slowly over a long span of time.

In a society based on speed and productivity, moving slowly is a radical act. We get so caught up in moving at a fast pace because of a fear of falling behind. We do not realize how the need to rush is often self-imposed. We are partially motivated by what we think others are doing, but these thoughts are not fully based in reality. They are largely the creation of our own imagination. Our human habit has an attachment to hierarchy and the desire not to be at the bottom of it. The perception of hierarchy is something that we even impose on growth, healing, and wisdom as we measure ourselves against others to see "who is better" or "who is ahead."

The attachment to speed and hierarchy is a sickness of the ego. There is nothing wrong with having goals and accomplishing great things, but when we are primarily consumed with being ahead of others, we are no longer working with a balanced mind and we are causing ourselves suffering through the process. Is it really a win if all the way through you suffered under all this self-imposed mental tension? Working and creating without attachment, making things for your own good and the good of others, moving without strict time limits, finding the balance between being committed and not causing yourself tension—this is how the brave and wise move through life.

When the body is tired, the mind can quickly get defensive. When we repeatedly push ourselves to get a lot done, we forget to prioritize proper rest. Getting caught in a cycle of constant productivity uses up our inner reserves and sometimes even pushes our mind out of balance. The tension in the mind that builds up from exhaustion can easily morph into narratives of worry or into fake stories that further agitate the mind. When we are tired (or hungry), it is easy for the mind to jump to conclusions or lose its patience with other people. There is nothing wrong with working hard and being effective, but make sure you are nourishing your well-being by making time to rest. When you respect your need to rest, your journey forward will be much smoother.

●

manage your reactions by slowing down
listen to your intuition by slowing down
restore your energy by slowing down
enter the moment by slowing down
feel your truth by slowing down

Moving at Your Own Pace

As I started getting more serious about meditation, I made a few friends around my age who were also going to the same meditation center. They had a similar dedication and a deep commitment to liberating themselves from all ignorance, misery, and old patterns that kept them in a self-destructive loop. I was so inspired by their efforts because they were attending retreats back to back and making a lot of time to serve retreats as well. I would go to the center a few times a year to meditate or serve ten-day courses (serving is when you support those who are meditating by making their meals), but my friends never really left. Every few months, when I would return, they seemed wiser, calmer, and more in tune with the truth they were able to access in the body.

Though I was seriously inspired by their mental strength to put themselves through such a transformative process over and over again, I also felt pangs of jealousy and a bit left out. I wanted to be free, too, and I knew that freedom takes real work. Why was I not living at the meditation center, as they were, and moving on the path at such a serious pace? I honestly felt a lot of tension and doubt about how I was going about things, and I felt a strong craving to do more. But when I checked within myself to see if I had more mental space and energy to sit and serve retreats more often, I really didn't. I felt like I was getting more than enough from going to retreats a few times a year and from sitting for two hours a day at home. Doing more simply did not feel right. The transformation I was going through felt deep enough and the changes in my perception made me feel that I had my hands full. I was learning so much, but I instinctively knew I needed time between retreats to digest it all and fully internalize the new insights.

I had to reconnect with humility and embrace the fact that my pace is my own—I had to recognize that the amount of time I was spending in retreats each year was as much as I could handle. I also had to accept that I had responsibilities, outside of meditation, to my wife and my family. Over time, I have realized that dedication is not measured by how hard you go or the intensity of your practice. It is measured by your ability to stay committed to the journey no matter how long it may take. My conditioning could handle intensity, but it also needed slow moments to be able to process how much I had really let go. Moreover, I felt a strong pull to set aside time to pursue the new aspiration that meditation had helped me uncover: an undeniable urge to write.

I did not realize then how much I was failing to appreciate my journey and how comparing myself to others was making me doubt my progress and commitment. It was wonderful having so many friends who were practicing the same teachings as I was, but I needed to work at my own pace and not compare their journeys to mine. There is so much power in having healing companions, people who can share the ups and downs of your inner journey, who know the path you walk on and support your inner successes, who can have discussions about new insights that are bringing light into your life. These are priceless people who fire up your inspiration so that you can continue trudging through the mud and breaking new ground within your own internal landscape. But what is essential to understand is that your fellow explorers are each healing at their own pace. Keeping the pace that works for you ensures that you will move at a sustainable rate, meaning that you will be able to delve deeper and your journey will be more fruitful.

Competitiveness has a tricky way of sneaking into every facet of life, even into our healing journey. Craving will make us want to feel what others feel, to overcome big issues and hit new heights of happiness in small amounts of time, but real healing has nothing to do with speed and it most certainly has nothing to do with comparison. Noticing these tendencies within ourselves and bringing ourselves back to the critical understanding that our journey is personal, intimate, and unique will help us regain our balance and reconnect with a sustainable growth rate.

Growing sustainably means knowing yourself and how much you can handle. It means having a clear balance between doing deep work that brings up a lot of old things you need to process and creating ample time for rest and integration. If we keep digging deeper and deeper, without time for rest and ease, we will force ourselves into a constant state of discomfort and create conditions for us to fall out of balance. If we push ourselves too hard, we may fall into exhaustion and want to stop the work altogether. When it comes to healing yourself, maturity means not bringing up so much at once that it overwhelms your mental space. You don't want to shock your system by overloading yourself with a multitude of past trauma and emotional history. Each one of us carries so many patterns of dense conditioning that we are better off seeking small internal victories as opposed to dealing with every issue we have all at once. Even though our issues are incredibly interconnected, there is nothing wrong with trimming the weeds so you can clear your view and then gather your strength to fully pull out the roots that cause you so much misery. Building up your self-awareness so you have a clear idea of how much you can handle will help you stay balanced.

Integration periods are a key part of moving at your own pace. The amount of wisdom you can gain from going inward is powerful and awe-inspiring. It can shake you to your core and completely shift the way you see yourself and the world. Spending time with truth is incredibly transformative, and truth will not just speak to you and give you lessons—it will ask you to embody the teaching and carry it with you wherever you go. Accepting all that you are, loving the hard parts of yourself, meeting yourself with gentle compassion, and bringing this higher degree of self-awareness to your life will cause radical shifts in your personality and behavior. Making time to settle into the new you is necessary if you want to make your long journey sustainable. Letting what you have learned settle into your perception takes time and intention. Making space for yourself to find and explore your new rhythm while you review what you have learned is foundational work that sets you up for future success in your growth.

Reflections

What was a challenge that surprised you once you started your healing journey?

Can you remember a time since your healing journey began when you were proud of the way you handled a tough situation? How was the way you handled it different from how you would have in the past?

What is your relationship to your identity now? Is there more space for it to be flexible?

What are some old pieces of wisdom that used to serve you well but do not quite fit your life at the moment?

Are you respecting your need to rest? Can you notice when a slow moment is upon you and embrace it, as opposed to resisting it?

Have you gotten used to moving at your own pace when it comes to your healing journey?

How have your preferences changed since your journey began? Have you had any trouble letting go of the old you?

How do you handle your storms? What is it that triggers them? Do you have resources or techniques available to help you through them?

Chapter 9

Internal Changes Ripple Outward

When your mind starts connecting with your human nature more easily, real-life changes start happening. It may start off slowly at first, but, in time, the changes multiply and the impact of your inner work becomes undeniable. How you see yourself and the world may shift so much that you start to feel as if you are living a new life, as if a rebirth has taken place. One of the biggest leaps forward is when your perception becomes less driven by old, tough emotions and more focused on taking in what is actually happening without making harsh judgments.

To be able to see and live with a fresh mind that is no longer in survival mode is a gift that we can only give ourselves. Being diligent about your introspection will activate an inner transformation that will make everything good inside you expand and empower the wholesome qualities that support your well-being to take charge and become the dominant aspect of your mind. When you are going through a moment of revival, there is no use hanging on to the old you. You can only do justice to your evolution by moving in the direction of your flourishing and by being okay with letting the shell of the old you crack and crumble away. The challenge of this grand expansion is releasing your attachment to who you were and boosting your courage to accept your natural unfolding.

Creativity

When you can connect more deeply with your human nature, your mind will have a greater sense of clarity because it is not as focused on the past. This ability to take in a fresh view of things will help you solve old problems in new ways. The feeling of being stuck and caught up in a recurring problem is often driven by our inability to see the situation clearly. When we keep looking at ourselves and our life through the dense lens of the past, it is difficult to come up with new strategies to remove these blocks from our lives. The more you can be in the present, the more powerful your mental clarity will be. This clarity can help you see more than your own perspective and allow you to be open to the flow of creativity. Inner peace and mental clarity make a powerful combination that produces an immense amount of original and imaginative thinking. Some of the best insights emerge when the mind does not feel rushed and can patiently consider a topic. A mind that is relaxed is open to insight and it can connect the dots of your previous knowledge to create new perspectives. Life-changing insights are not forced, they arrive in their own time. All you must do is focus on being and observing.

Creativity is the spark of inspiration that allows new ideas to come into existence. Creativity is most powerful when we are no longer far away from ourselves, when our internal connection with how we feel is strong and open. Creativity requires energy, and normally our energy is consumed by worry, anxiety, fear, or mental turbulence. When the mind develops harmony and is less overrun by the programming of old human habit, it more easily dwells in a relaxed state that has abundant energy. When the mind connects to the present moment, it is quite energizing because you aren't getting caught in old narratives. This is why meditation feels so restorative: You are practicing being aware and present. Whether you are aware of what is happening within you or what is happening in front of you, there is intentional presence that helps you stay open to any creativity that may arise.

When the mind is no longer overloaded with mental burdens, it can look at the world in a new way. Internal changes that arise from intentional healing affect our personal lives, but they can also have a huge impact on the world. Healing opens the door to happiness and creativity, and not just for people who are artists. Anyone, in any field, who takes their healing seriously, will be able to bring new insight to their work. Creativity and courage have a strong relationship: It takes bravery to develop something new and put yourself out there in a way that deviates from the norm. Creativity also compounds as it scales up. Not only will scientists be able to make new discoveries, teachers will create better pedagogical methods, and so forth. People will collectively have the courage to say no to old ways and bring forth new ideas for creating a more harmonious society. Imagine the type of political and economic solutions that will emerge from the millions of people around the world who are actively healing themselves.

New Boundaries and New Actions

A strong need for boundaries will feel natural once your healing is underway. The emergence of the new you will be fragile at first—it will need fortification and space to fully mature. Boundaries will play a big role in giving you the shield you need from the world as you go through your metamorphosis. A boundary is a form of protection that helps you stay aligned with who you are becoming. Think of boundaries not just as a way to reclaim your power, but as a way to intentionally design your life. Once we start observing ourselves, we will see that a lack of boundaries made life harder in the past.

Taking your healing seriously makes you more selective

about who you give your time to. The people you are around will undoubtedly affect you. Moods do not just sit within us. They impact our thoughts, words, and actions, and set the tone for the energy in a room. Not only should you be aware of the energy you are giving off, but you should also recognize the energies that you are allowing into your space. Ultimately, it is your perception and reactions that condition your mind and have the biggest impact on how you feel, but you do not help yourself by entering environments that feed old patterns you are working on breaking. Distancing yourself from situations that weigh you down is essential if you want to protect the new you that you are in the midst of cultivating. You can do this in a way that lets you honor your truth while not being rude, by saying, "I'm sorry, this is not for me" or "That wouldn't be good for me right now." As you continue reaffirming your inner wholeness, what people say or do will have less of an impact on you. Being able to move through life while staying in alignment with how you want to feel and behave is a sign of great maturity.

Building boundaries that are useful in the moment and checking in with ourselves to reassess and change them as needed are essential to this process. Building boundaries is different from building a wall. A wall can easily become a block that keeps us from evolving and learning how to deal with difficult interpersonal situations, while healthy boundaries will support our well-being. A wall is a long-lasting attempt to run away, to shield ourselves from difficult feelings, but a boundary is a temporary need for space that morphs as your inner world matures.

There is nothing wrong with defending yourself and removing from your life those who cause you harm, but it is ultimately impossible to remove all challenges from our lives. Our energy is best used trying to enhance our patience and problem-solving skills so that we can solve issues whenever they arise. Each individual will have to find their own balance with boundaries, to see where they are needed and where they are excessive. No one knows your life the way you do and no one will know your needs at any given time unless you make them clear to yourself and to those in your proximity. You have the right to design your space in a way that helps you thrive.

When you start connecting with yourself, the way you handle your friendships will be transformed as well. Improving your ability to be honest and vulnerable with yourself will tighten and deepen your inner circle. Your boundaries will help you bring new energy to the connections that you truly value. Cultivating a connection requires time and intention, which means that superficial connections will be left behind. Not because you are rude or mean, but simply because a single human being only has a finite amount of time. Especially in a world that is normally so fast-paced and technologically demanding, we only have so much energy we can give to others. The important thing is that you will finally be able to give attention to the friendships that matter to you so they can fully blossom.

Your inner circle will be composed of people who have a rejuvenating presence, who are radically authentic, who you can share laughter and truth with, and who support your growth. Your friendships are a critical investment. They are the network that can uplift you during hard times and share your joy when you succeed. Your relationships with different friends will evolve as you continue growing. No one individual will give you everything you need. But you will have more conversations that leave you in awe, that shift your perspective, that inspire you to take action, and that remind you why life is a miracle that you should use to the fullest. Your own self-awareness and growth form the foundation, but your friends are the pillars that hold up the roof of your home.

The changes in your mind and heart will reverberate outward into all facets of your life. First it will start within you, meaning your perception and your relationship with the ups and downs of your mind and life. Then the changes will trickle out into your inner circle, even if the people around you are not trying to intentionally transform themselves. The shifts in your behavior will make old, long-lasting relationships feel new, and, when you change the way you behave with those closest to you, those shifts will cause them to reassess how they want to respond in turn. Sometimes people will fear the changes and other times they will be inspired by your growth and find the changes refreshing, which helps them muster the courage to step outside of how they normally used to do things with you.

My relationship with my father changed immensely once I started going through my own transformation. The two of us were always close, but there was a distance between us because neither of us had a strong connection with our emotions. Our relationship was real, but it could have benefited from more depth. His love for our family has always been profound; however, he mainly showed it through how much effort he put into making sure that we had a home and food. My father was the one who brought our family to the United States; he led the charge so that our family could take a leap forward. And I never doubted his love for me—it was evident in how tirelessly he worked so that we could have our immediate needs met.

When I started healing my mind and deepening my connection with truth, I found so much love and gratitude for him and all that he had done for us. And I knew that the mix of him having a tougher childhood than I had, combined with the uphill battle of being a poor immigrant, had hardened him over time. He did not express his love for us too often and he was not one for many hugs. Soon after I started meditating, I mustered the courage to try to change the patterns in our relationship. One day, when he came home from work, I gave him a big hug, and that hug was the start of hugging him more often and telling him that I love him.

The love I was giving him softened his walls, which had built up over time. He started telling me he loved me as well and slowly revealed more of his story. My expression of vulnerability changed our dynamic. He began opening up and it felt like he became much more authentic and even more youthful. Not only did he start hugging me, but he started hugging others in our family and telling everyone he loves them. He did not feel the need to quietly carry the burden of his down moments alone anymore. A hug and three short words forever changed our relationship. They opened so many new avenues of depth and, to this day, our relationship continues to flower as we figure out life together.

The interesting point—and I've seen this repeated many times in my own life and with others—is that everyone in your closest circle does not need to intentionally undergo an introspective healing process for your relationships to start changing. If you take your healing seriously, the way you engage with your inner circle will become much more authentic and you will have more courage to live your truth. Those who are open to your new actions may take them as a sign that it is okay for them to be more open and that it is also safe for them to be vulnerable with you. Granted, some may be confused or put off by your authenticity, especially if the relationship they have with themselves is too distant. Ultimately, if they really love you, they will accept you as you move through the different stages of your healing evolution. They will recognize that you are in the midst of blossoming into your best self and they will happily support you. A change in your actions has the power to set off a chain of events that breaks the patterns you formerly had and opens up the space between the two of you. Love flows more easily when honesty and vulnerability are welcome.

Community

The next circle that feels the waves of your transformation is your community, which includes the local spaces you inhabit and the work you do for a living. There are many people you interact with in this wider space. Some of these interactions you enjoy and some of them you may find difficult. One of the biggest things we get from introspection is a greater sense of compassion for others that emerges from understanding how our own story has influenced our patterns. The Buddhist nun Pema Chödrön once said, "Compassion is not a relationship between the healer and the wounded. It's a relationship between equals. Only when we know our own darkness well can we be present with the darkness of others. Compassion becomes real when we recognize our shared humanity." Having our own understanding of how difficult life can be—and how that difficulty impacts the way we perceive things and behave—activates a new compassion toward the people we interact with. Even in those we dislike, we can see that their patterns must be coming from somewhere. Perhaps behind the hard and unkind exterior there is some trauma or tragedy that is driving their survivalist and selfish behavior. Not only do we develop more compassion, but we also bring less tension to our interactions with them, which will inevitably make the encounters better for everyone involved.

When we lessen the load that we carry in our minds through self-healing, we usually end up having more energy for life. In our community, this can mean we have more mental space to take part in activities that align with our newly discovered values and aspirations. Since we are less far away from ourselves, we can now come closer to our community, take direct action, and do our part to help mold it. When we see our personal struggle, we also start seeing that each individual carries their own burdens as well. The mix of new energy and compassion invites us to look at our surroundings and find a path that we can take to help alleviate suffering.

Conventional Truth versus Ultimate Truth

A rise in inner wisdom causes massive waves of change in our perception of ourselves and the world. The greatest truth that opens the door to happiness is the undeniable role that change plays in all of existence. The more we understand change, the happier we can become. Most of our old inner struggles revolved around our superficial understanding of change—we saw it as something slow and outside of us, without realizing that it is the fundamental essence of who we are. Without change, nothing would exist, and because of change we have the opportunity to temporarily *be*. Change allows the existence of human life itself. The truth of change lies at the core of the human condition. Not only are we rapidly changing at the atomic level, but all aspects that compose our mind are in a state of movement. Anything that is moving is in a state of change. If you take this truth to subtle levels, it reveals that who we are is a momentary construction, a series of rapid combinations that come together to create the image of our existence. We are an amalgam of great complexity, moving at incredible speed. To ourselves we feel real, but the true nature of our reality is fundamentally in flux. Which one of your atoms is you? Which constantly changing mental state is you? Which fleeting experience is you? If you were to pull all these aspects apart, which one of them would be you? Our existence is more akin to a moving river: Though the river is there, it is in a constant state of transformation. By the time you point to one part of the river and say that it is the river, the rushing waters will have already changed. Human beings have that same property, even though it is hard for our eyes and minds to fully grasp this concept.

The truth that who we are is not fundamentally substantial or static, and that our ego is incredibly fleeting and illusory, may feel daunting. The ego screams and says, "Surely

I exist." Having to always buttress who we are, to defend the image we hold in our mind, is a constant source of stress. "I" is helpful at the conventional level because, yes, you and I are here and we have to deal with the realities of everyday life. But at the ultimate level, "I" is not real, and letting go of it within the quiet of your mind actually opens you up to the flexibility that you need to cultivate real peace. Letting go of "I" will open you up to your real strength, to the finest qualities that the human mind is composed of. What the Buddha called the "heavenly abodes," or the "Brahma Viharas"— the qualities of love, compassion, sympathetic joy, and equanimity—flourish and expand in the absence of "I." Love is so powerful that it even has the capacity to protect you—the true power of love will not let you become a pushover. A person with real love beaming from within will take the necessary actions to protect themselves whenever necessary, and they will do so without having hate in their mind toward their aggressors. They will simply do what is necessary to defuse the situation. Harmony begets harmony, even if it has to take serious action to do so.

Even though we are a constantly moving composite of mind and matter that has temporarily coalesced, our conventional existence has real ramifications. At the ultimate level, we don't fundamentally exist, but at the conventional level, we do. Both of these things are true; our two levels of existence do not negate each other. Being able to live in balance with these two truths can help us let go of so much misery related to our sense of self. The narrow and unkind perceptions people may hold of us will have less of an impact on our mood. Wanting to be seen in specific ways will feel less important. Wanting to compete and move up the imaginary social ladder feels less critical. And what does feel more important is living a life of authenticity. The idea of "I," when it becomes too large, makes us narcissistic and self-centered. "I" makes it easier to twist logic so that we can feel okay about behaving in unkind and selfish ways. The opposite is the diminishing of "I"; when we grow in selflessness, connecting with others becomes easier, and love becomes more possible. We feel less stress to enlarge our sense of "I" and more of an easy focus on living in a wholesome manner.

Balancing the conventional truth, of living life among our family, friends, and communities, and the ultimate truth that we ourselves and everything around us is a series of rapidly changing subatomic particles moving in and out of impermanent combinations, may initially feel tricky. But with time and intention, we will be able to use the ultimate truth of change to relieve the stressful pressure that rapidly adds up at the conventional level. When we only think of reality as the life we live at the everyday level, we quickly get bound up in the illusion and lose the wisdom and nourishing effect that the truth of change can bring into our lives. When we become less attached to "I" and understand that we, the observers, are also an impermanent phenomenon, we can flow with greater alignment and gain more wisdom as we move through this beautiful opportunity called life.

Be the river and flow.

Moving Outward

The last circle that is affected by your transformation is the world. Even though you are one among billions, your thoughts, words, and actions create waves that are felt through the collective of humanity. The change in you is also a reflection of what many others are going through. This global burst in introspective work is not just happening within a few people; it is happening at a tremendous scale. Jiddu Krishnamurti, a sage from the modern era, once said, "A change in one is a change in millions." This current time, when therapy and meditation are rapidly spreading through the world, puts an exclamation point on this idea. History will take note of this moment, when countless people are going inward to address their past and their inner turmoil so they may come out as freer and happier versions of themselves. Internal changes that are multiplied by millions will have an undoubtedly powerful effect on the world. It is already proven that when people move together, history changes—the civil rights movement in the United States is one of the clearest examples of this point. Now we will see what the impact of people moving and healing together will have on the present and future of humanity. My hope is that this new wave of change, spurred on by our healing, will help establish the foundation that human dignity requires for all people around the world—meaning an end to starvation and extreme forms of poverty, access to health care, and great schooling for all.

When your mind starts beaming with more love for yourself and others, when compassion blooms strongly in your heart, when your perception is no longer governed by the past, and when clarity feels more readily available, it is natural for the way you see the world to shift in radical ways. Love is a powerful force that brings harmony into your being. It motivates you to treat others with gentleness and to do what you can to bring harmony into the lives of others. Love does not ask us to exhaust ourselves, but it does ask us to serve where we can and to offer our skills and energy to support others in living well. A lot of the harm we are aware of in the world once felt tolerable because we ignored the hurt we carried in ourselves. It was easy to think that this was just the way things were because we had no clear ways to help relieve us of our own conditioning. As we gather the courage to find our own way through our wounded forest and remove the layers of sedimented conditioning that block the light of our human nature, we get the firsthand experience we need to know that change is possible. Once we see that inner change is real, it makes the idea of outer change seem much more achievable.

When you look out at the world after your transformation, with new eyes that are clear and full of compassion, you notice that things are out of balance and that there can be much more kindness in the world. Not just between people, but between people and the structures that we have created. Your self-love and growing compassion will connect you with your voice and help you see that you are much stronger than you formerly thought. This process of introspection will not only give you the courage to change your life, but it will help you have the courage to walk alongside others and work to build a better world.

One huge challenge in building a better world is a selective form of compassion from people involved in large corporations as well as governments. In some areas they present themselves as moralistic, but in others they turn a blind eye to the harm they are willfully causing and blame the system they are a part of, instead of wholeheartedly committing to the values and kindness that they would like others to treat them with. What's interesting is that, in some situations, even when individuals hold themselves to a higher standard, once we start working in large groups, we accept structures that are less supportive of our collective well-being. As individuals we try hard to be kinder, but as groups we too easily throw kindness out the window. Groups of human beings tend to place the responsibility for making change on others.

This shifting of responsibility becomes a never-ending cycle, resulting in no real change occurring. To break this cycle, we need to take more personal and collective responsibility.

We know that compassion among individuals is real, but the task of our generation—the healing generation—is figuring out how we can take that interpersonal compassion and scale it up to the structural level. Love motivates the creation of more love. If more people become guided by love and seek to use their lives to bring more harmony and peace into the world, it becomes possible to create new systems that aren't privileging the few on top and unfairly treating everyone below. We need to be bold with our love and let it guide us to create a world that is defined by its structural compassion.

Reflections

What new aspirations have risen up from within you since you started your healing journey?

Have you changed the way you show up in your family? At work?

Have your views of the world shifted? In what ways? Has the growth of compassion inside you made you believe new things in a way that would have surprised the old version of you?

How has embracing change impacted your life and the way you see yourself? Does it make the process of letting go a little smoother?

Do you see yourself as static or dynamic?

Since your healing journey began, how has your relationship with your ego changed?

Chapter 10

Harmonizing the World

I grew up in an area of Boston called Jamaica Plain. Before it was gentrified, most of Jamaica Plain was a very diverse, low-income community. My neighborhood was primarily composed of people from different areas of Latin America. Almost everyone around me was working class, and very few were middle class; wealth seemed like something distant that could only be seen on TV. Even my high school, Boston Latin Academy (not to be confused with the wealthier Boston Latin School), was at the time known as one of the most diverse schools in the country. Even though I was an immigrant, I didn't feel like an "other." Many of my classmates were also first-generation Americans and were dealing with the same stresses and money pressures as I was.

The extremes of the world weren't clear to me until I entered my first year of college at Wesleyan University. I knew the small-town setting would be different from Boston, but, aside from that, I honestly had no idea what to expect.

And Wesleyan has a beautiful campus, like something out of a movie. But pretty quickly I went from noticing all the nature to picking up that most of the people around me were white. This, in itself, wasn't shocking, as one of my best friends from home was white, but he didn't have his own private plane. That a few people in my dorm had actually arrived in a private plane blew my mind and opened up my eyes to the fact that this place had more wealth than I had previously thought possible. When I started looking for a part-time job on campus, I realized that I was the only one in my hall who was even looking for one. No one around me seemed to be worried about money or the loans that were mounting up as each semester passed. What came to sting even more than the differences between my bank account and those of my classmates was how disadvantaged I was in terms of education. Many of the people I went to college with had attended elite private high schools that gave them a huge head start at Wesleyan. I almost always felt that I was lagging behind, and it was a continuous struggle to keep up.

I love the people I went to college with. I met my wife and most of the friends I am closest to today during my time at Wesleyan. So I would never change that aspect of my history, and I don't harbor any resentment toward them because they are simply the product of their environment. Nor would I change where I went to high school, because that space cultivated the drive I needed to get into a college like Wesleyan. Living through that disparity for four years was transformative, and it showed me how out of balance the world is. These experiences gave me a clear picture of the extremes that exist in the world. In some ways, it feels like there are two worlds—one space where it is natural for people to struggle with money issues and receive a lesser education and another, smaller space where money is never a problem.

It is easy to see the lack of balance in the world and get stuck pointing fingers. What would be much more helpful is to understand why things are the way they are and start moving toward changing them. A lot of individuals get stuck playing parts in harmful systems, but blaming individuals won't change the systems themselves. A more successful approach is taking a macro view of how the world is shaped and moving as a collective to redesign society. Before we can mindfully and intentionally work toward harmonizing the world through the creation of structural compassion, it is necessary to understand our current collective problems and their connection to the human mind.

The ancient phrase "as above so below" is especially relevant when trying to understand how society is structured. The world we live in today is created from the sum total of humanity's inner beauty and inner roughness. *Our world is not an accident. It is a reflection of humanity's current level of maturity.* And the primary obstacle to reaching structural compassion is the ego—and the division and hierarchies it creates. A better world is not possible without a vast healing movement to help stabilize society.

The survivalist mind is often self-centered, and its sight is narrowed down by two primary motivators: craving and aversion. Though the two fill the mind with massive amounts of tension, we stay in this loop of struggle because our past reactions keep reinforcing this conditioning. Until we do our inner work and discover our human nature, it is difficult to react with anything other than ceaseless cravings and the fears those cravings produce. Craving and aversion are the children of ignorance. We each exist and make decisions based on imperfect information. Human beings are limited by perception. We cannot immediately assess things fairly because we have to use our intention to remove the past that colors our perception—we have to teach ourselves to be more objective, as opposed to being driven by emotional reactions.

Ego inherently generates friction. It makes us see our fellow human beings as competitors, and forces us to create mental hierarchies in which some are above others. We design in-groups and out-groups as defensive measures, even when there is nothing for us to be defensive about. Ego creates situations where we struggle for power, as opposed to working together for the greater good. Whether it is about where we stand on the social ladder of our family or community, how much wealth we have, or how intelligent or wise we seem, compared to others, ego keeps the mind trapped in imaginary comparisons that take up much of our mental energy. Alas, what begins in the mind as imaginary takes real shape in the world through our actions—molding and shaping society to reflect the unevenness and fears in our minds. Ultimately, our collective egos create systems that, over time, harden into institutional forms of harm.

Ego controls our minds through the assumption of scarcity. It pushes us to compete for prized positions in our communities out of fear that we may be left with nothing if we do not comply and play the game. Ego emerges out of the craving for survival. Living through a lens of survival not only makes for an inner world riddled with suffering, but it imposes a similar type of tension on the external world. The harsh and unforgiving patterns of the mind have taken concrete shape as the rigid external divisions that keep us from living well and living as free people together.

Ego has a volatile and combustible nature. It sways between extremes. It can feel immense greed toward something one moment and then quickly flip and feel aversion toward something else. Whenever we come in contact with anything, we quickly evaluate it. Our perception is constantly deciding if something is good or bad. This constant state of assessment, which is driven by what we have experienced in the past, stops us from observing reality clearly. Observation is not the same as judgment. Observation is an act of presence, combined with selflessness, where you suspend your views so you can objectively take in what is happening. By contrast, judgment stems from taking in the information you're receiving through the slanted views of perception, as influenced by the ego. Normally, our assessment is charged with reactive emotional energy. If our identity comes under attack, our ego roars with defensiveness and fills the mind with tension. It seeks any maneuver that will help it protect its real or imaginary influence in our life.

If we were to only focus on creating change in the external interpersonal space that we all share, we would never address the roots that our society stems from—the individual. If we want to heal the world, not only do we have to redesign society, but we have to aid individuals in healing the things that push them into causing harm. A prominent American meditation teacher, Joseph Goldstein, once wrote, "On the deepest level, problems such as war and starvation are not solved by economics and politics alone. Their source is prejudice and fear in the human heart—and their solution also lies in the human heart." Individual healing and global change have to move together as one, if we want to successfully forge a new global peace. If we are able to decrease the amount of trauma and hurt that people hold, peace will start to flow more widely in the world.

Good people who uphold great values and want to see positive change in the world are often thwarted by their own unhealed pain and reactive patterns. When your emotional history is unknown to you, it can flare up and consume your actions when life gets challenging. Even when you lift up the banner of hope, it is easy to drop it when you have never taken the time to go inward and untie the roots of craving, aversion, and ignorance that manipulate your mind.

One of the biggest problems that humanity has come across again and again is that we want a better world, a healed world, but our leaders and the masses are not themselves healed enough to produce that new world. Often, in our attempt to produce a better world, we end up re-creating the harm that we were actually trying to eradicate in the first place. Especially if that movement to create a better world starts gaining energy and momentum, the flaws of unhealed egos will start to appear. If craving is still rooted in your mind, it has the potential to dominate your actions and cause harm. *Power functions like a magnet that reveals your roughest patterns.* Like throwing kindling on a fire, power will often fuel the self-centeredness of the mind.

Ego Creates Triangles

If you look at the shape of society from a design perspective, you will notice that our governments, businesses, wealth, and power take the form of a triangle, with a handful of people at the top who make decisions for the masses at the bottom. The deeply ingrained attachment to hierarchy that every ego carries has helped organize society so that a few have great power over the many.

The ego loves centralized power, especially if this structure works to its benefit. Even though many people are capable of exceptional leadership, how things are structured does not allow most to have the opportunity of exercising their skill to shape the groups they are a part of. Some assert that the triangle shape affords great efficiency to any organization. This may be true to a certain degree, but it comes at the cost of blocking the power of those who are not fortunate enough to land one of the coveted spots. Those who do not end up at the top of the triangle naturally feel disenfranchised and oppressed.

There is another argument that says people can simply start their own company—that's the way to become the boss and be at the top of the triangle. But that only solves the problem for a handful of people, because, once again, they design a company in the shape of a triangle where they have the power over the fate of many. The major problem of the triangular shape of society is that it breeds animosity and friction. No matter who is at the top, those who are not in control will feel the effects of their disenfranchisement and experience a growing resentment for the rich and powerful, especially when material inequality is so glaring.

Even if you think about it in terms of social movements and revolutions, once the oppressed acquire power, they often take revenge on those who once oppressed them in the name of justice. Justice is too easily confused with revenge. Harming those who have once harmed you generates a cycle of violence and simply creates more resentful people who may seek revenge on you at a future time. If groups of people are constantly battling for power and taking revenge on their former oppressors once they win, social friction will continue to get in the way of harmony and a long-lasting peace. People will often seek power and then get stuck in the same dynamics they were trying to change. The cycle of harm will continue until we address the root cause of suffering within the individual.

Healed Human Nature Creates Circles

Our next version of global society has to be more empowering, and to make that a reality we need to design our organizations to be more flexible. To disperse power to more of us, we need to start thinking in more circular ways, where power and wealth are more equally shared, as opposed to just trickling upward into the hands of a few. Circular designs already have a degree of popularity through cooperatives, worker-owned businesses, mutual aid funds, and horizontally run organizations. The way to a better distribution of wealth and power is not a mystery—there are already proven models that people are successfully utilizing.

The circular model of society calls us to evolve our idea of democracy, to deepen it so that more people can create and vote on laws. Having very small groups of people who have such an outsized impact on our collective future is a recipe for dissatisfaction and harm. Involving more people in our local and national democratic governance will have a healing effect on humanity. From my own experience, I've seen how people become activated when power is distributed more equitably. The organizing I've done with the BYOP, and later on in a group called Youth Against Mass Incarceration, showed me how much people appreciate being part of making big decisions—and they often end up growing through the process. In BYOP, we would spend time talking about different issues in our schools or city that we cared about. We would then decide among forty or so people during our citywide meeting what we actually wanted to work on. When there was a clear majority, we would start strategizing for our new campaign. What I saw from my peers was that, because we collectively decided what we would work on, everyone felt a sense of ownership over the campaign, which made people more excited to be part of the movement. Not only did we give direction to our work, but we built deep bonds with each other. People from different parts of Boston, who would have not met if it were not for this space, ended up developing lasting friendships.

Being part of a process that helps you live in your power is deeply transformative. I remember when I first met my friend Corina: She would come to the BYOP meetings, but was shy and quiet. As time went on, and as she was given more responsibility, the leader in her awakened. In the group, she ended up becoming one of the people everyone went to for guidance and inspiration, and now, as an adult, she carries herself with a mix of boldness and grace. Being part of a democratic process that was highly circular played a key role in her evolution.

If we can speak to each other and find that there are ample similarities in the things that we desire, we will be able to humanize each other in our minds. It is easy to dehumanize someone when you don't know their name, story, or family. We can combat alienation and revitalize our communities by giving people power over their community. Allowing the public to decide how government funds will be spent in their communities is called "participatory budgeting." This is a clear way of deepening democracy that gets people more involved than just voting every few years. We should not only bring back the town hall, but we should also give it power. You are less likely to harm your neighbor when you know your neighbor.

The only way to create a more humane society is by making sure that there are many options of how things are designed. If people are happily functioning within a triangular structure, then they should not be bothered. But if people want to create new groups and institutions in circular models, society should support them. What matters is that people are voluntarily in the situations they are part of. As humanity matures, our task is to expand the number of opportunities that are available to all of us. If others are looking for more opportunity to exercise their power, there should be avenues for them to do so. What matters is that we act on our ideas and that society supports us in their creation. We should be free to do as we please, as long as we are not harming others in the process.

Balance Instead of Extremes

A common reaction to change is fear, and for some people this reaction is even more pronounced when we are talking about creating change in society. A positive change does not need to be scary, especially if it is tempered and suggested with the understanding that it serves humanity best to move away from extremes. Allowing ourselves to fall into extremes is what got us to this current state. Any changes to help build a better future should be made with balance in mind. Balance in this sense is compassion for all involved in hopes of elevating the situation into a new degree of harmony. When we look at any major global issue, we should act on it with a heart that hopes to bring more love into the structural design of society and with a mind that seeks balance instead of extremes.

It is undeniable that we are experiencing a climate emergency due to our collective impact. Though the idea of increasing climate instability is daunting, this struggle is also one of our biggest opportunities to redesign how we function as a global people. We need to address this problem from all angles—not only by creating truly clean sources of energy and reining in the immense amount of fossil fuel emissions by corporations (research by the Carbon Disclosure Project found that 70 percent of emissions are created by just one hundred corporations) but by enhancing our idea of what "empowered care" looks like when disasters strike. For example, if we can handle destructive weather events with a greater amount of compassion—so that impacted individuals continue being cared for, even after the cameras go away—it will show that our compassion is real. Love does not just appear when things are hard. It is there before hardship strikes and remains after it is gone, because it takes time for people to get back on their feet. Hopefully, our innovations can lead us to build circular economies that are less wasteful and no longer dependent on endless growth models. We can only extract so much from our planet. If we push our home to an extreme, it will no longer be able to nourish us.

Racism and patriarchy need to be directly combated with compassion. These two societal ills have caused enough damage and division. Leveling the playing field for all people does not mean that our goal is to force everyone to be the same. The real goal is to set people up so they can actually play on the field. This is not about creating new and unfair advantages; rather, this is about correcting historical trends that continue to unfairly stratify society. Those who are not in oppressed groups normally fear that a push for more justice, equality, and inclusion means that those who normally did not benefit from the structure of society will turn the tables and become the new power-holders, lording it over those who previously held the reins of power. This is far from the truth. The old game of some controlling others has to end if humanity wants to be successful in the long run.

War is one of the clearest signs of immaturity. The slaughtering of many for the gains of a few is a tragedy that has traumatized humanity throughout history. Reacting through violence for the sake of control and ego games weighs our collective down. Addressing disagreements without violence is a critical threshold that we need to cross if we are to truly think of humanity as civilized. It is possible to hold a disagreement within a container of compassion, so that all sides are heard and a new harmony is created. For this to happen a paradigm shift needs to occur where a critical mass of people profoundly understand that human life is absolutely priceless and that society should revolve around supporting the thriving of life even when different powerful groups disagree.

Another great challenge in front of us is making sure that the online future we create is actually serving us, instead of hurting us. Unchecked algorithms that have no sense of morality or compassion for the user can create incredibly harmful results. The last thing we need is our technology amplifying the rough and heavy aspects of our character. If the online media that we use to connect with each other are insidiously enhancing our craving and placing us in tiny bubbles where we only see our own preferences, we will not only deepen our mental tension but curtail and slow down our personal growth. Online human connection can be a critical tool to help us build a better world if we use it to elevate instead of to denigrate. Social media is simply a reflection of ourselves. It can show us our roughness or it can show us our love. We need to make sure that we humanize current and future online platforms by imbuing them with compassionate forms of design. Our tech should connect and inform us without making us addicted or lonelier. All platforms should intentionally create their product with the well-being of the user in mind.

We are not trying to create another extreme where few exert power over the many. The love that grows within us calls us to simply make society more fair so that all people have what they need to flourish and live their lives as they wish. Just as it is in a relationship between two people, so will it be in our great collective. Our goal is to support each other's happiness. We cannot make each other happy because that comes from within. But we can observe the conditions of the moment we are in and make the adjustments we need, so each other's happiness becomes a greater possibility.

The ego loves when other people think the same way it does. It craves similarity. But this is in direct conflict with freedom. We need to teach ourselves to have the mental agility to appreciate a diversity of views. Groups of human beings come up with great solutions when we do not have the same views at the initial stage. We share what we know and have clear exchanges, so we can then come up with a better plan. Letting our egos control how we view the world will not help us, because the ego is normally in survival mode, and that is not where we are anymore. *We are trying to enter into an era of compassionate abundance, where all can share in the great wealth humanity has created.* Rising above ego and thinking from a place of compassion will help us honor our responsibility to ourselves and our families. At the same time, it will allow us to think in more complex ways, so that we can simultaneously act on a greater vision for humanity as a whole.

Our greatest hurdle will be the ego's fear and desire to control. Fear keeps humans from wanting to share abundance. Our addiction to control makes us fear that if we try to take care of everyone in the world, we will have to surrender our own freedom and our own resources. The truth is actually the total opposite. It is hard to be fully happy for yourself and others when there is so much suffering around you. If we work together to alleviate that suffering, our collective environment will feel lighter. Things won't be perfect, but eradicating the hard material forms of suffering—like hunger, lack of housing, lack of education, and lack of health care—will certainly have a positive impact on everyone's well-being and conscious outlook. Taking care of each other will give us more freedom as individuals to focus on creating culture and art from the healed parts of ourselves. If outright survival is no longer our primary concern, we can bring our focus to the finer aspects of life and attempt to make our deepest aspirations a reality. Thriving is not only cultivating a healthy mindset, but bringing to life what you want to see in the world.

When you look at the world with honesty, it may feel overwhelming and you may wonder how you, as an individual, can help make the world a better place. You find where you fit into this movement by connecting with your interests. What does your ideal way of helping look like? If you are an organizer or entrepreneur, use your courage and creativity to build what you know is missing from the world. A new venture with a bold mission cannot help but attract like-minded people. We also don't have to start everything from scratch. With a bit of research, we can find out more about the areas we are interested in and give some of our time to already established organizations. *What matters is that you are finding a way to make your compassion active.* This will look different for everyone, but if more people try, humanity is bound to take positive steps forward. If one individual who changes themselves for the better creates a positive impact in the world, imagine what many millions of people can do when they work through the burdens that have been restricting them. Those who have taken their healing seriously build a better balance of compassion for themselves and others. They do not get caught up in extremes; instead, they give love and support when they can and are mindful to keep their own tank full.

Our challenge as modern people is to look beyond the superficial and see the subtle truth that carries more depth. On a daily basis, we are inundated with information that is narrowed down into bite-size pieces that are designed to make us feel certain ways. It is easier just to let your emotions be moved by the information you encounter, but that would be unhealthy and would not support your power. The digital world will play with the range of your emotional spectrum as if it were a piano. My wife likes to joke that she had to stop watching professional football and some TV shows because they manipulated her emotions too easily. Information is rarely presented objectively; it will come packaged within a narrative that is often hiding in the background. Information will be presented in a way that reduces its complexity and in a sensationalized tone for the sake of clicks and views. We live in a time when truth is scarce, but perspectives are abundant. Misinformation is rampant because attention literally creates profit. When you understand that your attention is precious and that the whole digital world is competing for it, you will be more careful with where you point your mind. You have to be critical and intentional if you don't want to be told what to believe—if you don't want to be digitally siloed and exploited.

An Essential Step Forward

One of the clearest places where we need to remove extremes and strike a balance is in the area of global poverty and wealth inequality. We live in an era when wealth has reached extraordinary and almost unfathomable heights. We need to straighten out our priorities by allowing our compassion to reaffirm human dignity. We need to focus our energy on covering the basics that human life requires. Food, water, work, health care, shelter, education, freedom—these are fundamental needs that we all do not yet have access to. Humanity will not be fully civilized until everyone has access to what they need to flourish.

There is nothing wrong with creating products and platforms that serve the public, but how we go about doing these things matters. People working in terrible conditions, working excessive amounts of time, and being paid unfairly for their labor is something that we need to leave in the past. A sign that humanity has really matured is people demanding and creating systems where the extremes of poverty are diminished to the point of nonexistence, where people are paid well for the work that they do, no matter what the industry. Our world needs a base level of humane treatment that should be denied to no one. Supporting human dignity should be our new imperative. We have the resources; now we need the will. There is nothing wrong with competition, but people should no longer perpetuate a system where there is the potential of going hungry, homeless, and un-cared for.

The wealth humanity created needs to be more evenly shared. This does not mean that people will lose the ability to create wealth and become financially successful. But it does mean that those who have extraordinary wealth have a responsibility to pay their fair share back to society in support of our collective uplifting. People fear communism and people also fear capitalism. To take any idea to an extreme, where you use logic that is devoid of love to reason out why it is okay to cause harm, is a clear sign that the path you have taken will end in ruin. What we need is balance. We need to draw what is best from our ideologies to find a middle path, a path that can take humanity to a new level of freedom and includes a global expansion of human rights. As part of this expansion, poverty should no longer be part of the story of human struggle. People should earn money at a rate that supports their independence and mobility. This doesn't mean making everyone rich. It means redesigning society so that all people are supported in their dignity.

Structural Compassion

Scaling up compassion from the level of the individual to the group and societal level is one of the key hurdles humanity has to overcome to claim its maturity. Structural compassion is the opposite of the structural harm that currently exists and is often ignored by society. Moving together to correct these societal ills and bring balance to how our governments, institutions, and businesses interact with people at large is the challenge that we need to face. Our maturity is not just measured by how we treat ourselves; how we treat others also matters. Currently, profit is one of the main forces that guides society on this planet, but our profit motive needs to be replaced with the striving to uplift human dignity. The common saying "People before profits" is something that we need to actualize, so that we can center human flourishing.

Structural compassion is a movement to redesign the world to better reflect love, as opposed to greed. Structural compassion is not a revolution, it is an intentional redirection of our energy so that more of humanity can live without such intense material struggle. Structural compassion is an attempt to build wider networks of support, giving people access to what they need and more opportunities for inner and outer success. Holding the vision of structural compassion as we move through the world will help us create positive shifts in the organizations that we are part of. Structural compassion is not a fight; it is a long-term vision that will be deployed through skillful and peaceful means. It is to everyone's benefit to build a more compassionate world, because when fewer people are hurting, everyone is safer and there is more victory, celebration, and joy. It is easier to feel at peace and be happy when you know that your human family is also doing well, in addition to yourself.

Structural compassion is an idea that we collectively have to define and turn into a reality. It is guided by the basic needs of all human beings. No one individual is going to come up with the exact way to accomplish this, and no theory or doctrine that currently exists will dominate how structural compassion should play out on the global stage. But there are a few clear questions we can ask ourselves that will show us if we are moving in the right direction:

Is this action decreasing harm?

Is this action allowing more people to share in prosperity?

Is this action supporting the freedom of individuals?

What other societal structures can we create to support human happiness?

Freedom is an especially critical component of structural compassion. We need to balance out the reality that human beings are unquestionably interconnected and that our existence is inherently collective. We don't just need each other, we *are* each other—and without each other we cannot succeed. It is no longer an option to ignore our collective nature and disregard the truth that what we do affects those around us. The pressures we've placed on the planet's health and its long-term viability have proven this most clearly. Our freedom is tied to our collective nature, and if we do not properly take care of the whole, the individual will not be able to thrive. If we ignore the suffering of many, suffering will come closer and closer to us until we, too, are consumed by it. If we truly want to be free, we need to see that we are one human family. If we take care of our family, then our happiness and ease will be able to reach new peaks.

We need to be careful that we don't take the idea of humanity as a collective to an extreme. We cannot become so focused on the collective that the individual disappears. If people cannot be themselves—if they are not allowed to create as they please, to work in the sectors that they choose, to benefit from their creations, to have the freedom of mobility—then society has failed. We all need to pay our fair share so that the greater good can be financed, and we need common societal goals that help us meet the needs of the many. But authority from above cannot have full control of our lives. If we cannot fashion our own lives, then we are no longer free. Authoritarianism is never the answer.

What we have seen happen in history is that freedom of the individual gets taken too far and the masses of people who suffer are ignored. On the other hand, the collective sometimes becomes the sole focus and individual rights start disappearing. We need to find a balance—in between the two, we will be able to build a stable and flourishing society. People are so diverse in their situations that we need individual freedoms as much as safety nets. We need to expand our compassion to encompass the world. This will help us identify with those we have never met but with whom we have so much in common. Our only real option to address the great challenges of this century is to fully recognize and act on the fact that we are all in this together.

Our intrinsic connection with other human beings becomes apparent when we are able to tap into our human nature with more ease. We see others and know that their story is not too far from our own; that we all struggle in our minds; that we all feel sadness, fear, joy, anxiety, and every other emotion on the human spectrum. We see others and know that life is never easy, that we all carry something heavy from the past.

A human being who takes their healing seriously becomes an agent of compassion. This does not mean that it becomes your sole purpose to help heal the world. But it does mean that you are open to helping alleviate the suffering in the world. This will look different for each individual. We all have unique capacities and responsibilities, but for many of us there is room to give more or even to join a group or movement that is trying to change the world for the better. Just as small acts of kindness make a difference, so do the small amounts of time that we give to larger projects that bring about direct change.

Harming others directly disturbs your inner peace. Not doing anything to help others when you know you can is also deeply unsettling. At our core, it hurts to see others struggle. Love has this incredible capacity to expand itself. It inspires us to create more love, to bring harmony to situations that we are part of, and to spread balance where we can. Love does not ask us to be endless crusaders—it simply asks us to help in ways that align with our talents and our means. There is nothing wrong with making it your mission to help others, but do not use it to escape whatever is happening inside of you. Even doing good work can be co-opted by the ego or by old pain. Our inner work must move alongside the work we do in the world; otherwise, we risk hitting the wall of burnout.

Humanity faces daunting challenges in this century: undoing racism and patriarchy, ending all forms of war, decreasing the harm of climate change, addressing the global income gap, and lifting up those stuck in the mire of global poverty. Fortunately, at the same time the largest healing movement in human history is taking place. The healing generation will continue to expand and take its place on the global stage. With greater access to the power of the human mind and our new collective energy, and with the abundant creativity that emerges from our true human nature, we will be able to push the bounds of what was once thought possible and bring a new balance to the world.

The challenges confronting us are formidable, but before you become overwhelmed by thoughts like "How can we ever fix all of this?" first look inward and heal your mind.

From the lightness of a healed mind will emerge a fountain of courage and creativity to help you look at old problems in new ways. We are at the beginning of an era of revitalization where humanity is connecting with an elevated form of creativity. Healing ourselves is the game changer we have all been waiting for—not just for our personal lives but for the world. It may seem counterintuitive, because we have the tendency to look outward for solutions to external problems, but our deepest potential cannot be activated unless we undo the patterns we carry and open up space in our minds so we can more gracefully enter any moment with clear presence. Healing is what will make a long-lasting future global peace a reality. Quietly, our deep-seated sorrow has always been our biggest impediment to building a better world. Until our own weight is lifted, it will create disarray, even when we wish to create balance. But we do not need to wait to be fully healed to take on the large external issues we face; the outer and inner work must be done simultaneously.

Reflections

What does structural compassion mean to you? In what ways would you like to see the world become more compassionate?

What is your relationship to the news cycle? Are you able to stay in touch with what is happening in the world without overwhelming yourself?

In what ways can you turn your compassion into action? Is there a movement or issue that you particularly care about? Is there an organization working on that issue that you may want to keep on your radar and support whenever possible?

How are you bringing compassion to your everyday life? Within your circle of friends? Family? People you encounter as you move through life?

If you were in charge, what things would you change about how the world currently works? If love were in charge, how would it redesign the world?

What problems do you see in society? Which ones affect you directly?

In what ways have you been part of the solution? In what ways have you been part of the problem?

Does your ego try to create hierarchies, even when you don't want it to? How do the tools you have gained from your healing journey help you reconnect with compassion?

What gives you hope that our world can be more humane in the future?

Chapter 11

A New Era

If you want to awaken all of humanity,
then awaken all of yourself.
If you want to eliminate the suffering in the world,
then eliminate all that is dark and negative in yourself.
Truly, the greatest gift you have to give
is that of your own self-transformation.

~Lao Tzu

There is nothing perfect about my life, but I cannot deny that there are clear changes in how my mind functions today as opposed to how it moved before my personal healing journey began. I still have down times, inner struggles, moments where my mind is full of tension. But, at the same time, there is more selflessness and a deeper ability to see things from the perspective of others. Compassionate thinking used to be completely foreign to me because I was too self-centered, but now I can more easily shift into a heart-centered approach. Ego is still there, but the truth of egolessness also sits comfortably beside it. Peace does not feel like an impossibility anymore—it is something that I am building on a daily basis whenever I meditate. I think that is how it goes for most of us: The path to a better life is a gradual one, where we sometimes feel as if we are standing in the middle of who we were and who we are becoming. We don't necessarily become enlightened, but we do become lighter. With enough steps forward, the past goes from being a heavy part of our life to an old memory that serves as a reminder of how much we have overcome. Personally, what matters most to me is that I am moving forward. Even if the steps are small some days, they still count.

Without this healing journey, yung pueblo never would have existed, and I certainly never would have reached millions of people across the globe. I find it interesting that the growth of yung pueblo synchronized with my personal growth. All of it grew slowly until I started meditating on a daily basis, and again there was another boost when I stopped taking all intoxicants. After I did my first twenty-day course, I was finally able to have enough mental stability to accomplish what I needed to release my first book. After I started doing thirty-day courses, things really took off, and the reach of my Instagram account grew exponentially. I have to be clear: I do not meditate to be a writer or to gain notoriety. I meditate so that I can take steps forward on the path of liberation by relieving myself of craving, but I cannot deny that meditating helps shape my writing and gives me a creative boost. I don't think you and I would be having this interaction at this moment if I had not stayed committed to meditating. I would have never been able to access my inner creativity without putting myself through the inner journey.

I've spoken in many different cities and have interacted with so many inspiring people that I know the healing journey is becoming massively popular. More and more people are jumping in and finding their own way because they, too, know it is time to do deep inner work. Countless others are going through the same process that I am going through. Their healing is awakening their power and they are using it for their own good and for the good of others. Real human nature is rising to the forefront of society through the hearts and minds of people who are healing. I find hope for the future in the people who are cultivating their ability to think and act through selfless love.

Priorities

The harmony within one person cannot do it alone, but the harmony within many will cause an undeniably positive wave of change. Don't exhaust yourself trying to change the world by yourself. No matter how hard you may try, you can't change the world alone. There is no individual out there who can fix everything for the rest of us. Bringing balance to our world has to be a collective effort.

The best thing you can do for the rest of us is to heal yourself. This is the priority above all else. Keep in mind that you don't need to be fully healed to be of service to the world. You can walk the inner journey and be a catalyst for change at the same time. As you move inward, your self-love will open the door to love for all beings, and that love will be active. You will be able to take action in a way that fits you well, plays to your strengths, and is in alignment with your talents and abilities.

Focusing on changing yourself is everything. When your mind becomes calmer, more aware, less tense, and better rested and nourished, your actions will become more skillful and a powerful creativity will emerge from your well-being. Life may become turbulent at times, but even if things get chaotic, do not abandon your healing. The wisdom you need to address the vicissitudes of life will emerge from the wellspring of your growth. Sticking to your healing journey will keep you on the right track. Lifting yourself up and addressing the turmoil in your mind will directly lift up the rest of humanity. Trust in the simple fact that, if your mind becomes less tense, you will be decreasing the amount of harm that can enter the world through you. As you increase your peace, it will add to the total sum of peace in the world.

Making yourself an agent of healing will remove you as

a potential point of harm in the interconnected web of humanity, and this is no small feat. It is actually one of the best things you can do for all of us. Removing your own potential to cause harm by filling your mind with love and learning to exist gently in our world is a deeply meritorious action. Living with a firm commitment not to cause other people harm will bring a bountiful stability to your mind.

Take your healing seriously and you will be able to imagine a better world. When you do feel that new love for the world, let yourself dream big and act on it. This is most certainly not the time to play small—that time is over. We need courageous answers for the problems our collective ignorance has created. Humanity stands at a crossroads, where we can continue shortsighted thinking and divisiveness or we can sow seeds of unity and start seeing our fates as deeply intertwined. We know we are capable of great things, as we have built a world of wonder, but now we must bring compassion to our society's foundation so that all may access the fruits of our individual and collective genius.

Courage

There will be many who will doubt that new great things are possible. Some may even doubt that inner change is possible, and there will certainly be those who think that improving the world is not realistic. Some people will hold tight to their limits and will let their unacknowledged past pain dominate their idea of what the future can look like.

In the face of this doubt, trust that what is actually unrealistic is keeping everything the same. Our task as the healing generation is to continue expanding our access to our human nature and not allow the negativity of those who are filled with doubt to stop our blossoming. We will have to be strongly determined, proclaiming within ourselves that, no matter what, we will move in the direction of healing ourselves and doing our part to help heal the world, even if some people want to stand in our way. This is a train that is heading toward a better future. People can join us if they wish; if not, we will simply continue our work through wholesome methods.

This is the moment when a vast portion of humanity is deciding that it is time to grow up. We need to take responsibility for the unequal and unsustainable design of society that we have consciously and unconsciously created. It is not all our fault; we inherited this world and much of the structure from past generations. But just as our mental pain is not all our fault, it is still our responsibility to accept it and heal it. In all truthfulness, we have no other choice but to accept this challenge. *Everyone who is healing their old trauma and learning to live beyond the past is part of the solution.* We can't expect perfection from anyone, but the commitment to our inner work will speak for itself. Out of it will emerge a new, more emotionally mature person who is open to their own evolution—a human being who holds a wider circle of compassion for themselves and the world. The ones who are no longer controlled by their blind reactions will be heroes.

A Loving Approach Matters

When so much is out of balance and many are suffering, it becomes easy for our minds to get trapped in a cycle of aversion. We may start to think that the only way to fix things is to cause a strategic amount of harm to those we may see as our enemies, but violence cannot bring about the end of harm. If we rely on violence, we will only create more wounded people who will later seek more violence as a form of retribution. This is a trap that humanity has fallen into countless times. Our primary tools to pull ourselves out of the quagmire of historical violence are love, forgiveness, and understanding. We need to fully embrace the truth that more violence will not fix anything. It destabilizes our minds and causes us to always look over our shoulders with the fear that someone may come after us the way we came after them.

●

In this world
Hate never yet dispelled hate.
Only love dispels hate.
This is the law,
Ancient and inexhaustible.

~Excerpt from the *Dhammapada*

If we want to build a better world, it has to be done through love. Love is the strongest building material in the universe, and unconditional love sees no one as an enemy. People fear love because they think it means you have to let people hurt you. This could not be further from the truth. Love is skillful; it supports us in protecting ourselves and it helps us protect others. Yes, we won't always get along and there will be times when we need to reorganize ourselves to make sure that all people have access to human flourishing, but this is not something to fear. Each new generation will have to make its own changes to continue enhancing human dignity and our collective quality of life. Love is open and it embraces change. It carries the quality of flexibility so that all may enjoy its fruits. We are not striving to build a utopia that will be perpetually perfect—that is not possible. We are simply striving to create a world where fewer and fewer people are hurting. The purpose of love is to remind us that humanity is a family.

Love cultivates essential qualities within individuals that we must try to implement in the structures of our society. Love is empowering; it supports freedom, and it encourages us to seek the understanding of one another. Love does not support hierarchies; it treats all people as worthy equals, and it seeks to nourish. Love does not seek to harm; it always aims to rise above division and fear.

We have two great objectives before us. One is beginning the healing journey as individuals and the second is coming together in groups to help design a better world that mirrors the qualities of love. Starting the healing journey is the hardest part, but continuing it is slightly less difficult because we see that our investment in our growth produces clear results. If we continue on this path, our life will benefit even more from developing inner harmony. The second objective is formidable because there is no clear path to building a better world. Our mission of decreasing global suffering is clear, but how we will get there must be navigated through a voluntary movement of people who share the same vision and values, people who understand the unquestionable connection between the healing of the individual and the healing of the world. Ultimately, the future will be designed by those bold enough to start modeling the world we want to live in without waiting for permission.

While there is no one path to building a better world, here are some guiding lights to help us see the way:

Selflessly listening to each other. Everyone has a perspective. We need to be intentional about placing ourselves in each other's shoes.

Sticking to our values. If what we are doing and what we are part of starts moving away from empowerment, love, and the goal of decreasing harm, then we are going in the wrong direction. Holding steady to our values will also help us avoid confusion when things get difficult. When we make a deep commitment to these values, our intuition will help us stay on track.

Honoring our perspective and ideas without becoming eternally attached to them. We need to leave space for nuances and have the humility to be convinced by better ideas. Humility will help us combat ego's urge to control. Ego often tries to convince us that our view is much more correct than everyone else's. When the mind feels superior, it means ego is winning. When the mind dwells in humility, it means it is open to positive expansion. As we move into building the future, everything will be situational, but our intuition and our values will let us know if we are doing our part to help ourselves and the world.

We should never allow ourselves to dehumanize each other. Often in history, before great harm was done to a group of people—or as the harm itself was being carried out—campaigns were created to dehumanize the oppressed group so that people could justify any harm they were committing. This is a pattern in human history that we must not replicate. The ego too easily falls into this trap of seeing some people as less than others, no matter how trivial the differences between us may be. Holding fast to our healing practices will keep us from falling into this insidious and sneaky trap of ego.

Expanding our sense of identity and allowing it to be flexible—to stretch over the entirety of the world so that we can see ourselves as integral parts of the human family—will help us move out of division. We should continue to honor our families, our histories, our nationalities, and all aspects that feel crucial to our identity. But to that we should add that we are human beings. We know this passively, but it is not something we fully live. Recognizing that people from all nations are our siblings will help us be more patient with each other when times are hard and support us in not going to harmful extremes. We do not need to erase our identities to see ourselves as a whole, but we do need to work together in a synchronized manner. If we let cooperation be our guide, instead of competition, we will be able to redesign society so that it becomes more circular and decentralized. This way more people can share in resources and decision making.

We fear change because we easily get attached to what we know, even if that knowledge is rough and fills us with dissatisfaction. In an insidious way, the things we know bring us comfort, even if we detest them. The fear of the unknown constantly stops great things from happening. Even if there is a real possibility for improvement, fear can become a block that stops any forward movement. Yes, there is risk involved—there always is, with every action. There is never 100 percent certainty, but are we really living if we let fear constrict our ideas and actions? Ask yourself: Are the ideas that you hold in your mind worth keeping there if they have not brought you real happiness? If your views of the world fill you with tension, then it is time to adopt a more hopeful stance that is open to good things happening.

Humanity and the world are begging for change. Change

from inside and out. Isn't it time for something new? Those of us who have been there know what rock bottom feels like, but we don't really have the option of waiting for the world and humanity to hit a collective rock bottom—that would be cataclysmic. Instead, we need to take responsibility for the current situation and lead with our growing maturity.

In the end we must remember that we simply need each other to thrive. We must act together with cohesion and with a mindset of solidarity.

Conclusion

Personal healing is possible, and I believe building a structurally compassionate world is possible. The two have an unbreakable connection and it all begins with you. As you make your mind lighter, the world will become lighter. So, find the healing technique that works for you—stick to it, dig deep, give it your time, let go again and again, be consistent, and do not worry if other people do not understand what you're doing. If your mind is becoming less tense and the intensity of your reactions is decreasing, then you are heading in the right direction. Your path will not be like anyone else's. Remember that whenever you doubt yourself, and keep walking bravely in the direction that enhances your peace.

Lead with kindness as you move through the world. You only truly know your own story; everyone else's, especially the stories of strangers you temporarily cross paths with, will be a mystery. Do the higher-level work of treating them with kindness. Kindness often has a disarming quality, even with people who act roughly. You can walk through our world gently, without letting people walk all over you or cause you harm. Kindness means leading with love. You will be surprised at how these small, wholesome actions of giving people your gentleness will support your healing and your inner peace. If you treat people well, your mind will have an easier time being calm because you will carry very little remorse or regret. It is not possible to have inner peace and be intentionally harmful toward other people. If we want to bring harmony into our lives, we need to intentionally sow harmony in the interactions that we are part of.

Help where you can, but don't overdo it. Find the movement or issue you deeply care about and give it some of your attention. Often this looks like donating, advocating, giving your time to an organization, voicing your beliefs, creating a new solution, or marching outside. There are a lot of ways to help; you just have to find a way where you are doing your part without overwhelming yourself. You can be part of the change without burning yourself out.

One of the biggest internal shifts that will impact the external environment is simply knowing that things can be better. If we center ourselves around a set of values—like the importance of self-healing, generosity, kindness, self-love, equality, and compassionate action—these values can function as a guiding light as we try our best to bring more harmony into the world. Wholeheartedly believing that compassion is possible on a grand scale will encourage more people to share in this mission. Eventually, this will cause shifts in the makeup of society. We have to believe it before we can build it. There is no one way to be an agent of change. We all have very different abilities. How you show up for the building of a better future will be unique to you. We shouldn't compete with each other to see who cares more about the world or who is doing the most impactful work. Our energy should go into supporting each other through this global healing process.

Don't let the ups and downs stop you from witnessing the beauty of life and partaking in its joy. For your personal life and for the world, these upcoming years will be important. Nothing about this journey that you have embarked on has been easy. Healing is the realm of heroes and every tough situation we go into won't necessarily end with a victory. There will be setbacks, tears, and heartache, but there will also be life-changing revelations, new freedom, and tremendous evolution. You and the world are bound to change. Set your intention to make sure the trajectory is aimed toward greater harmony. *Center yourself in your healing and everything else will flow from there.* The light that you uncover from within will show you what is important and where you need to go. Have faith in your ability to transform yourself and in the potential of the human family. We know we can change the world, not just because we can change ourselves, but because change is all there is. Your healing will create an opening to a better future. Free people living within the comfort of a caring society—once we arrive there humanity will no longer be young; we will finally be mature.

●

i commit to the inward journey
and aim to make my point and all my threads
in the web of humanity

full of self-awareness
full of compassion

with steady practice
i will patiently unload
the tension and burden i carry

knowing the more i let go
the less hurt there will be

feeling lighter and happier
i share my harmony with those i meet

Reflections

How will you continue making your healing a top priority? Are you committed to the long journey of healing your mind so you can live your best life and be an asset to the positive change our world needs?

What does your community look like today? Is there space within your circle of friends to support each other in your personal healing? Are you inspiring each other to grow into the best versions of yourselves?

How will you contribute to the building of a better world without exhausting yourself or becoming out of balance? Have you found the middle path where you can help others without hurting yourself?

Do you recognize how much power you really have? Do you still have further to go in terms of reclaiming your power?

How different are you now from when your healing journey began? Have you taken the time to truly appreciate how far you have come? Is there space in your life to celebrate the inner victories?

sending love to all

ABOUT THE AUTHOR

yung pueblo is the pen name of the writer Diego Perez and means "young people." The name is meant to convey that humanity is entering an era of remarkable growth and healing, when many will expand their self-awareness and release old burdens. He lives in western Massachusetts with his wife.

Wisdom and inspiration in poetry and prose from *New York Times* bestselling author yung pueblo

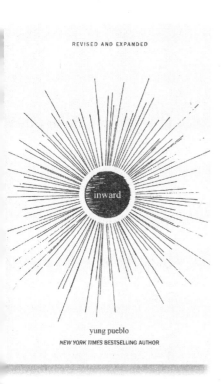

Inward considers the transition from self-love to unconditional love, the power of letting go, and the wisdom that emerges through self-knowledge. With an emphasis on mindfulness and meditative healing, it also implores readers to self-reflect and take steps toward finding their own inner peace.

Clarity & Connection explores how intense emotions accumulate in the subconscious and condition individuals to act and react in certain ways. Centered on healing within, it guides readers through the excavation and release of the past that is required for growth.

Available wherever books are sold.